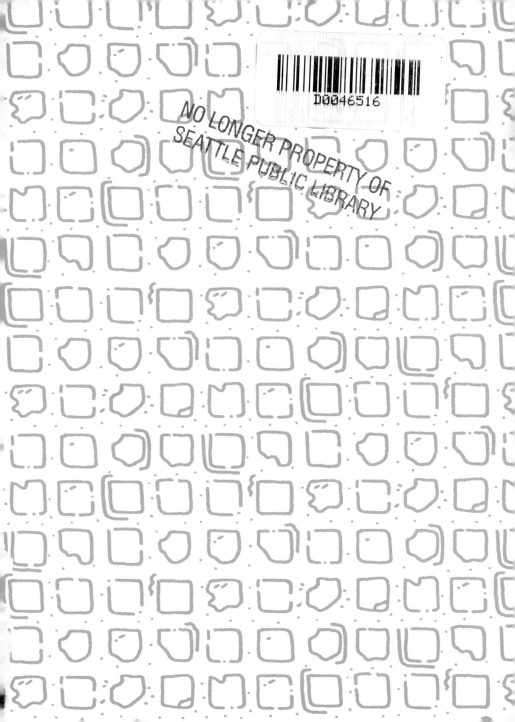

D0046516

SEATTLE WALK REPORT

SECRET SEATTLE

SEATTLE WALK REPORT

SECRET SEATTLE

An Illustrated Guide to the City's
Offbeat and Overlooked History

Susanna Ryan

SASQUATCH
BOOKS

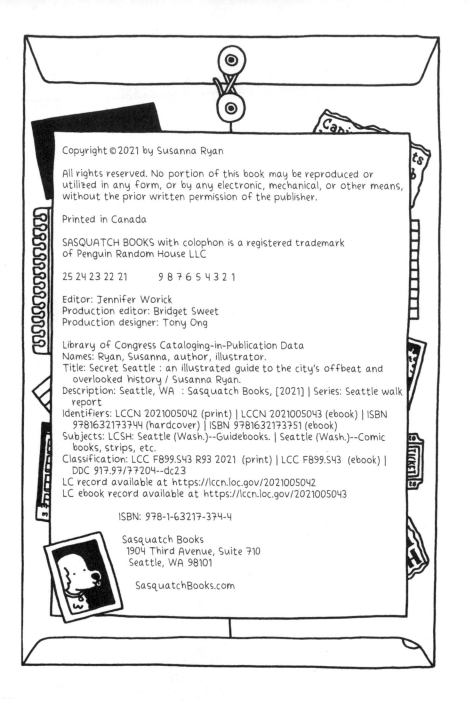

Printed in Canada

SASQUATCH BOOKS with colophon is a registered trademark of Penguin Random House LLC

25 24 23 22 21   9 8 7 6 5 4 3 2 1

Editor: Jennifer Worick
Production editor: Bridget Sweet
Production designer: Tony Ong

Library of Congress Cataloging-in-Publication Data
Names: Ryan, Susanna, author, illustrator.
Title: Secret Seattle : an illustrated guide to the city's offbeat and
    overlooked history / Susanna Ryan.
Description: Seattle, WA : Sasquatch Books, [2021] | Series: Seattle walk
    report
Identifiers: LCCN 2021005042 (print) | LCCN 2021005043 (ebook) | ISBN
    9781632173744 (hardcover) | ISBN 9781632173751 (ebook)
Subjects: LCSH: Seattle (Wash.)--Guidebooks. | Seattle (Wash.)--Comic
    books, strips, etc.
Classification: LCC F899.S43 R93 2021 (print) | LCC F899.S43 (ebook) |
    DDC 917.97/77204--dc23
LC record available at https://lccn.loc.gov/2021005042
LC ebook record available at https://lccn.loc.gov/2021005043

ISBN: 978-1-63217-374-4

Sasquatch Books
 1904 Third Avenue, Suite 710
 Seattle, WA 98101

    SasquatchBooks.com

CONTENTS

Dear Reader,

Five years ago, when I started taking long walks around Seattle for fun, it felt like the city was blossoming right before my eyes. Discovery awaited me at every turn, as previously ignored side streets were explored, Little Free Libraries were rummaged through, and spilled boxes of paper clips on the sidewalk became the catalyst for endless wonder. By slowing down and tuning in to my surroundings, I found myself appreciating the little things in life in a whole new way.

These strolls were turned into an online comic, and later, a book, called *Seattle Walk Report*, where the everyday mundanities of city life were meticulously documented through data collection and drawings. Even thousands of miles in, the ephemeral discoveries of a meandering walk were a renewable source of comic inspiration. But then, on a late summer evening in Capitol Hill, a new sort of inspiration struck.

I was walking on sidewalks whose every crack and contour I knew well, past buildings I had seen countless times, when something caught my attention. There, on the side of an old building on 14th Ave. and E. Pike St., appeared a small rectangular door at ground level. "CLARKS COAL CHUTE," an embossed emblem on the door read. "T.F. CLARK. PATENTED JULY 24 1906. SEATTLE, WASH."

Before I knew it, I was digging through US Census records, patent applications, newspaper databases, and photo archives, determined to piece together what I could about this mysterious man and his beautiful coal chute. A few weeks later and knee-deep in research, I returned to 14th and Pike in the daytime to get a photo of this object of my affection and... it was gone, the hole that remained covered up by a piece of plywood. A rented dumpster stood nearby. I felt like I had dreamt it (and briefly considered dumpster diving). This coal chute had likely been sitting on the side of that building for over 100 years, I'd spotted it, and then just weeks later, it was gone. What were the chances?

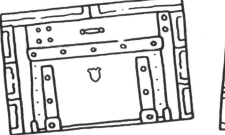 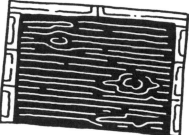

But then, I saw another Clark's Coal Chute on Capitol Hill. And another. My eyes were opened anew, and I began to wonder how much I really knew about the things I passed by every day on Seattle's streets, from light fixtures and utility covers to bricks and parks. The closer I looked at the parts of my environment I had glossed right over, the more questions I had. There was a heap of hidden history right under my nose, just waiting to be documented before becoming the next thing to meet its fate at the bottom of a nondescript dumpster on a Capitol Hill street corner.

(cue sad trombone)

GARBAGE
ONLY

On these pages, you'll find the untold story of T. F. Clark and his coal chutes, along with other tales—of trees, trails, and terra-cotta. I wanted to shine a light on the stories behind the places and things you can walk or roll by any day in Seattle, as well as share some of my favorite under-the-radar spots, most of which I didn't even know existed before a chance encounter on a neighborhood walk. My hope is that this book will inspire you to take a look at your surroundings with a new interest and curiosity. While mundane on the surface, a closer look may reveal some fascinating stories and secrets that deserve to see the light of day.

Love,

Seattle Walk Report
a.k.a. Susanna Ryan

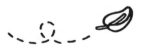

SPOTLIGHT on SEATTLE'S STRUCTURES

Pacific Science Center ✿ 200 2nd Ave. N.

Originally built as the US Science Pavilion for the 1962 Seattle World's Fair, the Pacific Science Center was designed by architect Minoru Yamasaki, a Seattle-born Garfield High School and University of Washington graduate whose body of work includes New York's original World Trade Center and Seattle's Rainier Tower. Instead of being torn down after the fair as originally planned, the science pavilion remained, and in 2010 the building was designated a historic landmark.

Union Station ✿ 401 S. Jackson St.

Today, Union Station is home to the headquarters of Sound Transit, but between 1911 and 1971 it served railway lines alongside the 1906-built King Street Station, which is only a block away. Union Station is open to the public during the day and worth a visit to admire its lovely interior.

Washington Hall ✿ 153 14th Ave.

Washington Hall was built in 1908 as a dance hall and lodge for the Danish Brotherhood fraternal organization and has lived on as a community gathering space for generations. Musicians including Billie Holiday, Jimi Hendrix, and Duke Ellington have jammed in this storied building.

INSPIRED by TRANSPORTATION

Pho Bac, 1314 S. Jackson St.
- ✓ Built in 1954
- ✓ One of Seattle's earliest pho restaurants
- ✓ Became an instant icon in the early 2010s, when it was modified to look like a boat

Orient Express Restaurant, 2963 4th Ave. S.
- ✓ Started as a diner with one railcar in 1949
- ✓ Additional cars expanded the restaurant, including some from Seattle City Light's Skagit River dam project and a car once used by President Franklin D. Roosevelt

3

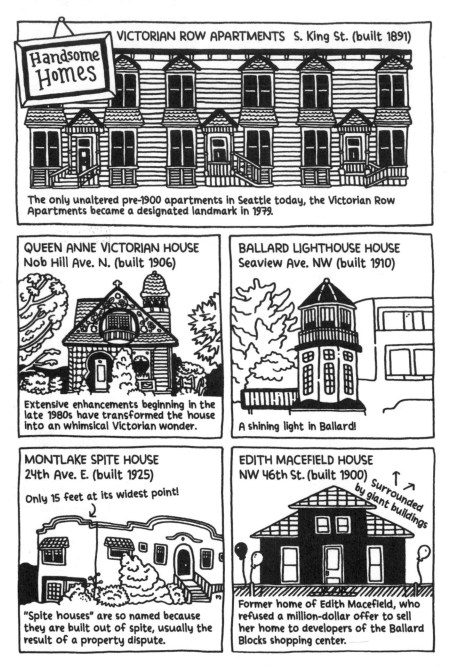

Handsome Homes

VICTORIAN ROW APARTMENTS S. King St. (built 1891)

The only unaltered pre-1900 apartments in Seattle today, the Victorian Row Apartments became a designated landmark in 1979.

QUEEN ANNE VICTORIAN HOUSE Nob Hill Ave. N. (built 1906)

Extensive enhancements beginning in the late 1980s have transformed the house into an whimsical Victorian wonder.

BALLARD LIGHTHOUSE HOUSE Seaview Ave. NW (built 1910)

A shining light in Ballard!

MONTLAKE SPITE HOUSE 24th Ave. E. (built 1925)

Only 15 feet at its widest point!

"Spite houses" are so named because they are built out of spite, usually the result of a property dispute.

EDITH MACEFIELD HOUSE NW 46th St. (built 1900) Surrounded by giant buildings

Former home of Edith Macefield, who refused a million-dollar offer to sell her home to developers of the Ballard Blocks shopping center.

COMPLAINTS ABOUT DIVISIVE STRUCTURES

Not all buildings are met with open arms. Here are some complaints about notable Seattle buildings from readers of the *Seattle Times* as plans for the structures were announced.

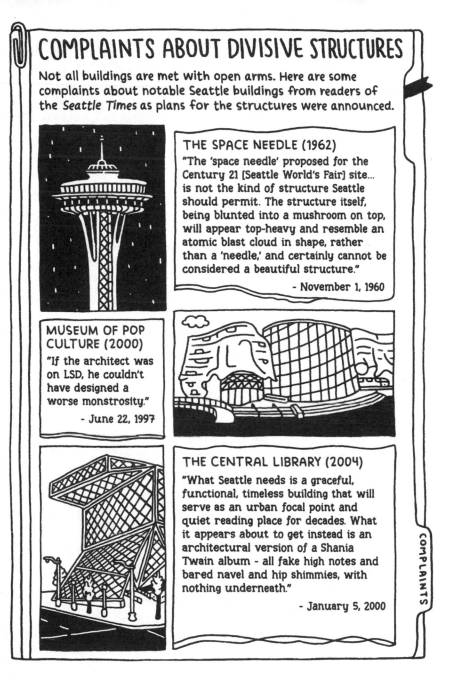

THE SPACE NEEDLE (1962)

"The 'space needle' proposed for the Century 21 [Seattle World's Fair] site... is not the kind of structure Seattle should permit. The structure itself, being blunted into a mushroom on top, will appear top-heavy and resemble an atomic blast cloud in shape, rather than a 'needle,' and certainly cannot be considered a beautiful structure."

- November 1, 1960

MUSEUM OF POP CULTURE (2000)

"If the architect was on LSD, he couldn't have designed a worse monstrosity."

- June 22, 1997

THE CENTRAL LIBRARY (2004)

"What Seattle needs is a graceful, functional, timeless building that will serve as an urban focal point and quiet reading place for decades. What it appears about to get instead is an architectural version of a Shania Twain album - all fake high notes and bared navel and hip shimmies, with nothing underneath."

- January 5, 2000

COMPLAINTS

The Chin Gee Hee Building

| 400 2nd Ave. Ext. S. | Pioneer Square |

HIDDEN GEMS

At first glance, the three-story brick-and-stone building at 2nd Ave. and Washington St. may not stand out from the other old architecture found in Pioneer Square, yet looking closer at its history reveals there is more to this structure than meets the eye. In addition to being one of the first brick buildings to be constructed after the devastating Great Seattle Fire of 1889 leveled 25 city blocks, it was commissioned by Chin Gee Hee, a prominent businessman and one of Seattle's early Chinese residents. Prior to the establishment of the Chinatown-International District, southeast of Pioneer Square, which we know today, Seattle's Chinatown was located on Washington St. between 2nd and 3rd Avenues. The Chin Gee Hee Building, which originally housed an import and export business and labor contracting company, is the last remaining building in the city's original Chinese district. A 1928 public works project to extend 2nd Ave. altered the shape of the building, but it is still a one-of-a-kind treasure with a connection to Seattle's past.

THE SECRET WORLD OF SIDEWALK STAMPS

In the early 1900s, sidewalks made out of brick and wood were SO last century. Concrete, with its unparalleled durability and longevity, was quickly becoming the standard material with which to build Seattle's walkways. At the time, it was common for the contractors selected for the job to stamp their work with the company name as a form of advertising and to commemorate a sidewalk well paved. Looking closely at the city's sidewalks today, you may come across one of these stamps, denoting a sidewalk only a few decades younger than the city itself. One hundred years and millions of footsteps later, the stamps serve as tiny tributes to the people who poured their hearts, and their concrete, into building Seattle's infrastructure.

TIPS:

Sidewalk stamps are more likely to be found in older residential areas that haven't seen as much development as other areas of Seattle, as construction often tears up sidewalks. When present, the stamps are almost always located at the beginning segment of a sidewalk, near a corner or intersection. If you suspect you see a sidewalk stamp but it's difficult to read, check the other side of the street. It is possible that the opposing sidewalk was paved by the same contractor and has a clearer stamp.

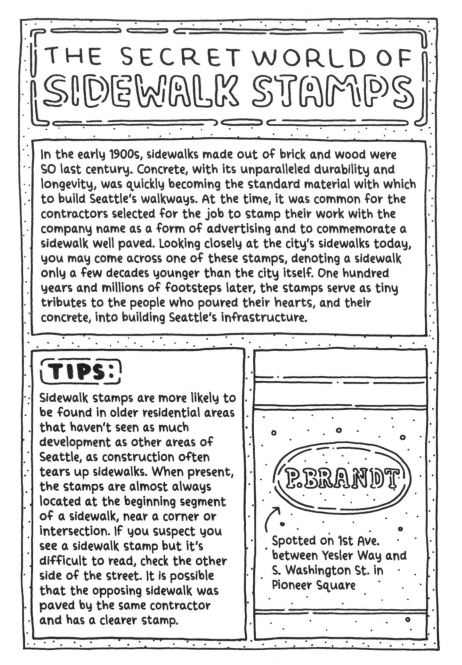

P.BRANDT

Spotted on 1st Ave. between Yesler Way and S. Washington St. in Pioneer Square

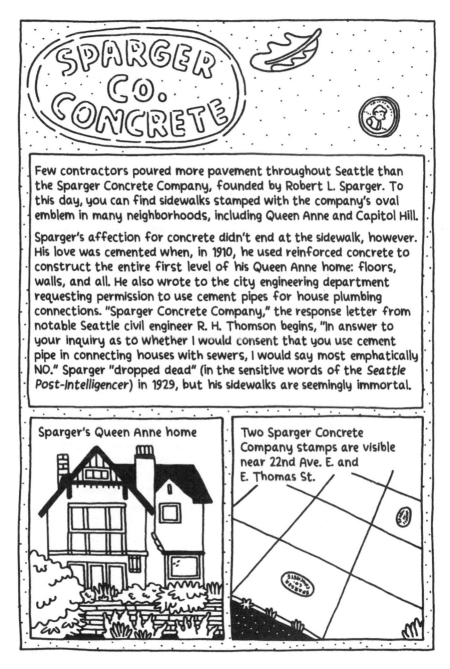

SPARGER CO. CONCRETE

Few contractors poured more pavement throughout Seattle than the Sparger Concrete Company, founded by Robert L. Sparger. To this day, you can find sidewalks stamped with the company's oval emblem in many neighborhoods, including Queen Anne and Capitol Hill.

Sparger's affection for concrete didn't end at the sidewalk, however. His love was cemented when, in 1910, he used reinforced concrete to construct the entire first level of his Queen Anne home: floors, walls, and all. He also wrote to the city engineering department requesting permission to use cement pipes for house plumbing connections. "Sparger Concrete Company," the response letter from notable Seattle civil engineer R. H. Thomson begins, "In answer to your inquiry as to whether I would consent that you use cement pipe in connecting houses with sewers, I would say most emphatically NO." Sparger "dropped dead" (in the sensitive words of the *Seattle Post-Intelligencer*) in 1929, but his sidewalks are seemingly immortal.

Sparger's Queen Anne home

Two Sparger Concrete Company stamps are visible near 22nd Ave. E. and E. Thomas St.

John Granger Peirce was the son of John Peirce, an infamous figure in Iowa history. The elder Peirce, a Civil War veteran, made his fortunes in Sioux City real estate before losing most of his money in the Panic of 1893, considered the worst US economic crash prior to the Great Depression. Looking for a way to settle his debts, he devised a plan to sell raffle tickets with his grand 21-room mansion as the prize, a successful scheme that led Peirce to sell over 40,000 tickets nationwide at $1 apiece (about $30 today). However, when New York millionaire William Barbour announced that he was in possession of the winning ticket, days after the Christmas Eve 1900 raffle drawing, the event was clouded in suspicion. In fact, Peirce owed Barbour money, and the deed to the mansion had been transferred to Barbour 19 days before the "winning" ticket was drawn. The raffle had been fixed to favor Barbour all along.

Eager to leave Sioux City behind and start anew in the West, the following year Peirce and his family moved to Seattle, where he and his son John G. Peirce worked together as general contractors. Within a few years, the younger Peirce married and started working on his own, first as an inspector for the city and later returning to the contractor business. He was appointed to the Seattle City Council in 1911 after a council member resigned due to illness, and when a seat was up for election the following year, Peirce decided to run. "Business interests of the city, knowing of his success as business man, and knowing of his integrity and high standing in the community... were urgent in their demand for his election," the *Seattle Daily Times* wrote in February 1912. Peirce won, only to resign two years later after it was revealed that he had sought illegal contributions for the campaign of Seattle mayoral hopeful J. C. Slater. Sidewalk stamps bearing the name "John G. Peirce" near W. Lee St. and the alley that runs between 7th and 8th Avenues W., in Queen Anne, mark Peirce's general contractor days, before his public fall from grace.

HANS PEDERSON

Even if you've never heard the name Hans Pederson, you probably know his work. As one of Seattle's most prolific contractors in the early 20th century, Pederson helped create the Arctic Building, King County Courthouse, Washington Hall, the Ballard Bridge, and Chinatown-International District's Milwaukee Hotel. Despite being referred to as King Hans by fellow Arctic Club members, he wasn't above taking smaller jobs, including sidewalk paving. And when he wasn't busy building Seattle, he enjoyed baseball. He was elected a director of the Seattle Baseball Club in 1931. Hans Pederson sidewalk stamps can be found throughout the city, like the one above, on Prefontaine Pl. S. in Pioneer Square, outside the Prefontaine Building, another Pederson creation. Talk about a guy who knew how to make an impression!

The Ballard Bridge

BALLARD BRIDGE

Hans Pederson

King County Courthouse

FRITCH & CO.
Spotted on 21st Ave. & E. Pine St. in the Central District

According to newspaper records, Fritch & Co. was primarily active between about 1897 and 1908, just enough time to make a mark on the Central District alongside this blue-and-white tile street label.

STIRRAT & GOETZ
Spotted on 18th Ave. & E. Alder St. in the Central District

Contractor Herman Goetz (1867-1941) was responsible for paving Seattle's first non-brick street, Union St. between 1st and 2nd Avenues, as well as installing the city's first sewers and water mains.

R.C. SMYTH
Spotted on 26th Ave. E. between E. Calhoun St. & E. McGraw St. in Montlake

R. C. Smyth was primarily known as a plaster contractor, and alongside fellow contractor J. J. Tinker created the decorative plaster work on Seattle's iconic Smith Tower.

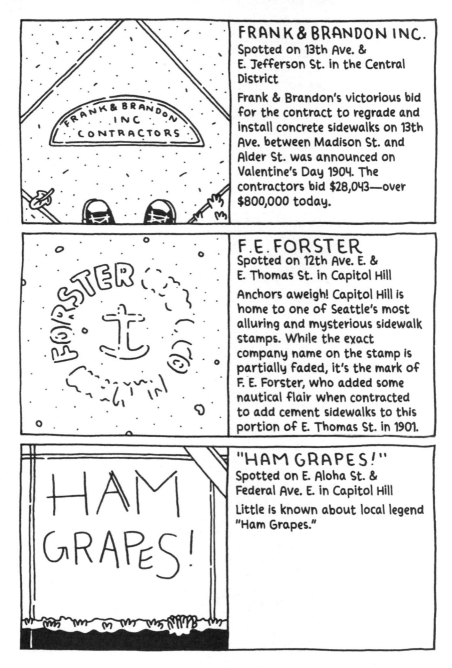

FRANK & BRANDON INC.

Spotted on 13th Ave. &
E. Jefferson St. in the Central
District

Frank & Brandon's victorious bid for the contract to regrade and install concrete sidewalks on 13th Ave. between Madison St. and Alder St. was announced on Valentine's Day 1904. The contractors bid $28,043—over $800,000 today.

F.E. FORSTER

Spotted on 12th Ave. E. &
E. Thomas St. in Capitol Hill

Anchors aweigh! Capitol Hill is home to one of Seattle's most alluring and mysterious sidewalk stamps. While the exact company name on the stamp is partially faded, it's the mark of F. E. Forster, who added some nautical flair when contracted to add cement sidewalks to this portion of E. Thomas St. in 1901.

"HAM GRAPES!"

Spotted on E. Aloha St. &
Federal Ave. E. in Capitol Hill

Little is known about local legend "Ham Grapes."

SOUTH SEATTLE COLLEGE
ARBORETUM
6000 16th Ave. SW

There is a lot to love at this 5.5-acre public botanical garden on the South Seattle College campus, from the wooden bridge surrounded by ferns in the Dawley Shade Garden to the peaceful stream that runs through the collection of conifer trees in the Coenosium Rock Garden and the nice city views from the arboretum's gazebo. The garden began in 1978 as the dream of horticulture students hoping to create an outdoor classroom, and it still serves that purpose today. It's also a quiet place for a wonderful afternoon walk (no green thumb required!).

Part of the Chinese Garden

Bridge in the Dawley Shade Garden

IT HAPPENED AT GREEN LAKE!

At Seattle's go-to walk spot Green Lake, there is so much more to see than dogs, daisy fields, and people attempting to Rollerblade for the first time in 20 years. Green Lake has a rich history, and clues around the lake reveal the beloved location's former lives that have made it a gathering spot for centuries.

As you stroll the lake, imagine some of the activities that have taken place over the years:

ICE-SKATING!

Although rare, Green Lake has occasionally frozen over. In 1929, eight inches of ice covered the lake, leading to a spectacular winter skate (and perhaps a sprained ankle or two).

HYDROPLANE RACES!

From 1929 through 1984, crowds turned out to see hydroplanes zoom across the lake, increasingly to the dismay of neighbors.

FIREWORKS!

From 1920 through 1979, Green Lake was a destination for Fourth of July fireworks. The show moved to Lake Union in 1980.

THE FUN FROLIC!

In 1921, the *Seattle Times* and Seattle Parks Department joined forces to host the first Fun Frolic at Green Lake and nearby Woodland Park, advertised as the "biggest play event ever planned for Seattle girls." Proceedings for the day included "costumes—all kinds," a doll contest, a brass band, and water baseball in the lake, along with a fairy-tale story hour. "It's the boys' turn to get jealous," wrote the *Seattle Daily Times*. The Fun Frolic was an annual event through the early 1970s.

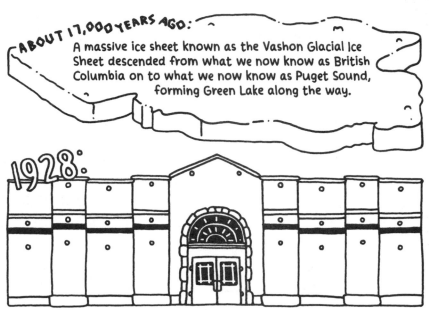

ABOUT 17,000 YEARS AGO: A massive ice sheet known as the Vashon Glacial Ice Sheet descended from what we now know as British Columbia on to what we now know as Puget Sound, forming Green Lake along the way.

1928:

Construction was completed on the Green Lake Bathhouse on the northwest side of the lake, a facility that included dressing rooms, restrooms, and lockers to accommodate lake swimmers.

Works Progress Administration workers built an artificial island on the lake, named Swan Island after a pair of swans donated by the parks department of Victoria, BC. Seattle city officials hoped the swans would start a permanent swan population on Green Lake, but that never happened.

1950 The Aqua Theatre, an open-air floating stadium on the south side of Green Lake, debuted as part of Seattle's first Seafair summer festival. A sellout crowd came to marvel at the Aqua Follies, a "swimusical" group that mixed water ballet, stage dancing, and comedy.

The Aqua Follies of 1950

GORGEOUS GEORGE

1961:

Famous professional wrestler Gorgeous George won a match against Leo Garibaldi at the Aqua Theatre, despite getting drop-kicked into the waters of Green Lake by his rival.

Leo Garibaldi

1962:

The summer of 1962 was a busy one for the Aqua Theatre as the Seattle World's Fair brought oodles of visitors to the city. Events included a three-day jazz festival, a week of performances by Bob Hope, several musicals, and, of course, the beloved Aqua Follies.

ANNIE GET YOUR GUN

THE MUSIC MAN

HA HA HA

1969:

In one of the Aqua Theatre's last hurrahs, Led Zeppelin performed at Green Lake only months after the release of their debut self-titled album. While some paid the $5 entry fee, others rented rowboats or camped out on nearby lawns to hear the band. It's possible that Led Zeppelin rocked a little too hard that day: city inspectors discovered damage to the aging outdoor theater shortly after the performance, and following one final show, by the Grateful Dead, in August 1969, the Aqua Theatre was dismantled, starting in 1970. The seating area on the south shore of the lake is the last remnant of this onetime theater.

Remnant of the Aqua Theatre

LED ZEPPELIN

SUNDAY, MAY 11, 1969
Aqua Theatre-Seattle
2:00 PM - $4.50 advance - $5.00 at door

1970:

SEATTLE
PUBLIC
THEATER

A Marriage Proposal

Anton Chekhov

While it was lights-out at the Aqua Theatre, it was a new beginning for the old bathhouse, which was remodeled into a 130-seat theater. The opening production included three one-act plays, including Anton Chekhov's *A Marriage Proposal*. Today the building is home to Seattle Public Theater.

SECRET GARDENS

Bradner Gardens Park: 1730 Bradner Pl. S.

This 1.6-acre park is a true community treasure that bustles with outdoor activity year-round. Not only does it contain a demonstration garden and a P-Patch, it's also home to a picnic shelter and a quirky collection of public art. This one is worth a special trip.

Parsons Gardens: 650 W. Highland Dr.

Small but mighty, Parsons Gardens is a sweet retreat in Queen Anne, teeming with a gorgeous assortment of flowers, plants, and trees.

Katie Black's Garden: 1150 S. Atlantic St.

Near this garden in Beacon Hill was once the mansion of Kate Gilmore Black, an accomplished musician and composer, and her husband, Frank Dewitt Black, a Seattle mayor who resigned after three weeks in office (ooh!). It is said that Mr. Black offered his wife a trip to Europe in 1913 but she chose to spend the money on developing a Japanese garden instead. Little did she know that this decision would be appreciated by Seattleites over 100 years later as they take peaceful strolls through the property, now a public park, which includes monkey puzzle trees and beautiful blossoms in the spring.

Shakespeare Garden: 901 12th Ave., outside Seattle University's Fine Arts Building

"I know a bank wheron the wild thyme blows..." Well, sort of. On the Seattle University campus, you'll find this literary-themed garden, featuring plants referenced by William Shakespeare in his plays, like thyme, tarragon, roses, and marigolds.

A rose by any other name would smell as sweet, but I still prefer the scent of cinnamon rolls!

CAPITOL HILL COAL CHUTES

A delightful remnant from Seattle's past that can still be seen today is the humble coal chute, a small, easy-to-miss door visible on the side of some of the older buildings and houses in town. Before natural gas or electric heat, many people used coal to heat their homes or businesses, and coal chutes were a convenient way for coal merchants to deliver this much-needed resource. Typically, these chutes would lead to a coal bin or a special room in the basement for storage. The use of coal declined rapidly in Washington State during the early decades of the 20th century as cheaper, more reliable options became available, and today, the coal chute is entirely obsolete. However, some buildings in Seattle are still rocking their chutes over 100 years later.

On a lucky day, you may stumble across one with a local connection: Clark's Coal Chute, manufactured in Seattle from 1906 until the late 1910s. In raised letters on a shield-shaped emblem, this coal chute proclaims a man's name: "TF CLARK." Who was this guy, confident enough to lend his name to many a coal chute door?

Theodore Farrand (T.F.) Clark

was born in New York in April 1847 and moved to Seattle in the 1880s, sometime before the Great Seattle Fire of 1889. At the time, whether you arrived in town before or after the fire was something of a pioneer litmus test, so in Clark's case, he was the real deal. A sheet metal worker, Clark set up shop in Seattle and became known for manufacturing portable camp stoves that would go on to be popular among the thousands of men flocking to Alaska with dreams of striking it rich in the gold rush. By the 1890s, he had married fellow New Yorker Mary Anne Semon and was living in Seattle's Capitol Hill neighborhood. He patented what would later become Clark's Coal Chute in 1906. In his patent application, Clark writes enthusiastically about the latest and greatest in coal chute door technology: this one has "*certain new and useful improvements*" and a "*neat and attractive appearance.*"

Clark also designed his coal chute to be "burglar proof," so would-be intruders couldn't slide into your house and steal your stuff, a surprisingly common problem of the coal chute era.

HEY KIDS! **CREATE YOUR OWN TURN-OF-THE-CENTURY SEATTLE COAL CHUTE TYCOON!**

Without any photographs of coal chute creator T. F. Clark, his appearance is up to our imaginations. What does *YOUR* dream T. F. Clark look like?

Select one of each to add:

(1) Steely stare!

(2) Mustache!

(3) Frown!

(4) Hat!

SO MANY POSSIBILITIES!

The coal chute appeared to be a hit. In a 1906 issue of the plumbing and heating contractors' trade journal *Sanitary and Heating Age* (a great beach read!), a piece about Clark's coal chute states:

"It appears that Mr. Clark first brought the chute to the attention of architects in Seattle last March and they pronounced it admirable, as is best indicated by the fact that a large number of the chutes have already been specified for new buildings... It would seem to have a remarkably bright future."

According to an advertisement from 1911, Clark had sold "over 1,400 [coal chute doors] in Washington and Oregon" between 1906 and 1911. Time marches on, though, and by 1920, Clark had given up his business, likely due to old age. He died on December 4, 1921, but some of his coal chutes—or at least their doors—live on to this day.

T. F. Clark's shop on Pier 50 in 1908

Shop on Western Ave. in 1917

It is unknown how many Clark's Coal Chutes were ultimately installed in Seattle or how many remain, but searching for them in neighborhoods with older buildings is a fun and satisfying pastime. No neighborhood appears to have as many intact coal chutes as Capitol Hill, though, where many fine examples exist:

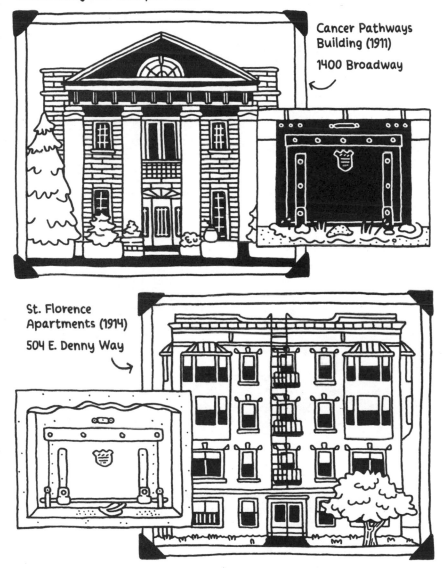

Cancer Pathways
Building (1911)

1400 Broadway

St. Florence
Apartments (1914)

504 E. Denny Way

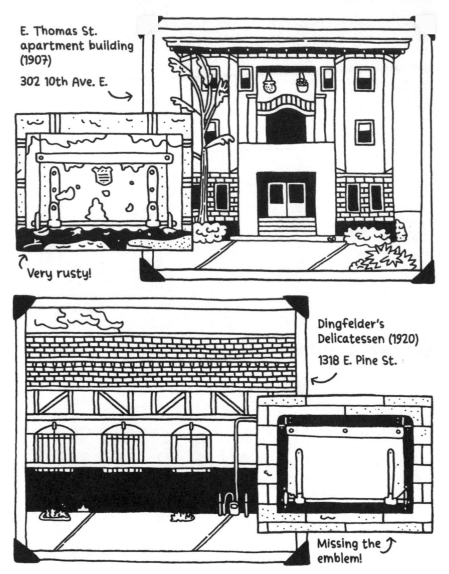

E. Thomas St. apartment building (1907)

302 10th Ave. E.

Very rusty!

Dingfelder's Delicatessen (1920)

1318 E. Pine St.

Missing the emblem!

TIP: Coal chutes are typically found at ground level on the side, not the front, of older buildings. They are often painted the same color as the rest of the structure and can be easily overlooked if you're not searching for them. The age of the building is the most important factor: if it was built after 1930, you are unlikely to find a coal chute.

THE **MOST EXCITING** COAL CHUTE ON CAPITOL HILL!

Buena Vista
Apartments (1907)

1631 Boylston Ave.

At some point, a standpipe was installed OVER the Clark's Coal Chute located on the side of this apartment building. It is truly something to behold, and a holy grail for standpipe and coal chute enthusiasts everywhere.

COMET LODGE CEMETERY

| HIDDEN GEM | 2100 S. Graham St. | Beacon Hill |

The only thing scarier than the ghosts said to haunt Beacon Hill's Comet Lodge Cemetery are the largely forgotten tales of the series of bureaucratic nightmares that brought it to be. Local legend has it that if you listen very carefully, you can hear the spooky sounds of unpaid taxes, shifting property lines, and deed deals, as well as eerie groans from the bulldozer that destroyed gravestones and threatened to bury the cemetery's history for good in the late 1980s.

Prior to the 1880s, the land in question was a burial ground for the Duwamish people. It then became the not-so-final resting place for some of Seattle's earliest non-Native settlers, including Emma Rigby, one of the city's first female doctors; Samuel Bevan, the last mayor of South Park; and, according to a *Seattle Daily Times* obituary, Modesto Reyes, who had the distinction of being the first person born in the Philippines to die in Seattle. By the 1930s, the cemetery was overgrown and dangerous, having fallen into disuse. In the decades that followed, some people made various efforts to clean up and restore the cemetery, while others made plans to develop the site into a park or housing. All the while, gravestones moved or went missing, records were lost, and property disputes dragged on.

Where once hundreds of gravestones lined the grass, few remain, yet against all odds, the cemetery still stands. The grounds inspire quiet reflection and the occasional ironic cemetery picnic thrown by teenagers, a small reminder that life goes on.

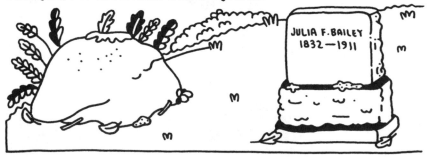

JULIA F. BAILEY
1832 — 1911

Pioneer Jacob Maple and his son Samuel were once buried at Comet Lodge Cemetery, but as the site fell into disrepair the ashes of their bodies were moved to their final resting place: embedded in a block of concrete on a patch of grass in the main parking lot of the nearby King County International Airport, a.k.a. Boeing Field. A small plaque there honors them.

People Honored in Seattle's Spaces

Dave Niehaus Wy S
Designated 2011 • SoDo

MY OH MY!

Longtime voice of Mariners baseball

J.P. Patches Pl
Designated 2013 • Fremont

Local children's television icon

Rev. Dr. S. McKinney Ave
Designated 2014 • Central District

OPEN HOUSING!

EQUAL RIGHTS!

Pastor of Mount Zion Baptist Church for four decades and civil rights leader

Speight Jenkins Wy
Designated 2015 • Lower Queen Anne

Longtime general director of the Seattle Opera and arts advocate

Alan Sugiyama Wy
Designated 2018 • Beacon Hill

NEWSPAPER

Lifelong Seattleite, educator, and community activist

E Barbara Bailey Wy
Designated 2019 • Capitol Hill

Bookseller and advocate of LGBTQ+ civil rights

30

Cal Anderson Park
1635 11th Ave. (Capitol Hill)

Washington State's first openly gay legislator

Alice Ball Park
8102 Greenwood Ave. N. (Greenwood)

University of Washington graduate and chemist known for developing a treatment for leprosy

Powell Barnett Park
352 Martin Luther King Jr. Way (Central District)

Community leader, musician, and baseball player

Donnie Chin International Children's Park
700 S. Lane St. (Chinatown-International District)

Neighborhood safety activist

Dr. Blanche Lavizzo Park
2100 S. Jackson St. (Central District)

Washington State's first African American female pediatrician

Victor Steinbrueck Park
2001 Western Ave. (Downtown)

Advocate for historic preservation, architect, and designer of the Space Needle

STATUES of NOTABLE SEATTLE MEN

1 Ken Griffey Jr.

2 Roberto Maestas

3 Rev. Mark A. Matthews

4 John H. McGraw

5 Dr. Robert W. Day

1 Edgar Martinez Dr. S. and Dave Niehaus Way S. • Artist: Lou Cella (2017)
Mariners baseball great Ken Griffey Jr. really hit it out of the park, scoring 630 home runs over his Major League Baseball career. He was inducted into the National Baseball Hall of Fame in 2016.

2 Near 16th Ave. S. & S. Lander St. • Artist: Casto Solano (2017)
Maestas was the founder of the nonprofit El Centro de la Raza and a member of the Gang of Four, a minority rights activism group in the late 1960s and early 1970s.

3 In Denny Park • Artist: Alonzo Victor Lewis (1942)
Reverend Matthews is considered by historians to be one of the early 20th century's most influential Pacific Northwest clergymen.

4 Near 5th Ave. & Stewart St. • Artist: Richard Brooks (1910)
The governor of Washington State from 1893 until 1897, McGraw championed the Lake Washington Ship Canal project, to connect Lake Washington with Puget Sound.

5 Near Ward St. and Yale Ave. N. • Artist: R. William Bane (1999)
The longtime director and president of the Fred Hutchinson Cancer Research Center, Dr. Day was instrumental in moving the center from its original home on First Hill to its current home in South Lake Union.

STATUES of NOTABLE SEATTLE WOMEN

(cricket sounds)

SYLVAN THEATER & COLUMNS
University of Washington Campus

Located next to the Paul G. Allen Center for Computer Science & Engineering, not far from Drumheller Fountain, on the UW Campus

Just off the University of Washington's beaten path, the four columns of the Sylvan Theater are some of the oldest still-standing architectural pieces in Seattle, dating back to 1861, when they were part of the university's first building in downtown Seattle. The stately columns have been in serene Sylvan Grove since 1921. Made of hand-fluted native Washington cedar, the four columns weigh a combined 4,000 pounds, more than the average car!

The Medicinal Herb Garden
University of Washington Campus

Located north of W. Stevens Way NE, between Benson Hall and the Chemistry Building on the UW Campus

At the UW's Medicinal Herb Garden, you can find over 1,000 plants from around the world. The garden, founded in 1911 by the university's Pharmacy Department, was across the street, behind Anderson Hall, before moving to its present location in 1939. Since then, between a lot of love and care and robust seed exchanges with botanical gardens from nearly every continent, the garden has grown to become one of the largest public gardens of its kind. With many paths to walk and plants to admire, it's the perfect campus retreat.

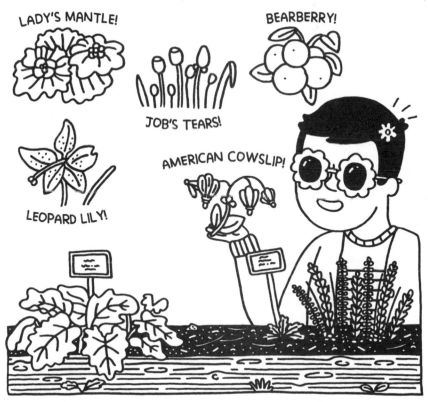

Agriculture in South Park

Many of the Pike Place Market's earliest vendors were the Japanese and Italian farmers of the town of South Park, who transported the fresh produce grown on their small farms to Seattle, often by way of a trolley that clanked over the nearby river's wooden drawbridge. Farming had been a rich tradition on South Park's land for generations: It was along these flat, fertile banks that the Duwamish people set up longhouses, grew crops, and caught salmon from the winding river now known as the Duwamish Waterway. Early white settlers also found the grounds most suitable for farming, and by the turn of the 20th century, the immigrants who would go on to grow Pike Place Market began calling the town home.

Pike Place Market was established as a way for farmers to sell directly to customers, bypassing the middlemen and produce commission houses that had for years shortchanged farmers and overcharged consumers. Initially, farmers were reluctant to bring their goods to the new open-air market, as commission houses had threatened to boycott those who did. Only eight farmers showed up to sell their produce on Pike Place Market's first day of business on August 17, 1907, but they were well rewarded: the customers turned out in droves, and before noon that day, there wasn't a single vegetable left. Word spread quickly. Two weeks after opening, those eight farmers had become a group of 70. With time, one South Park resident, Giuseppe "Joe" Desimone, successful both in farming and business, slowly began acquiring property at the market. By 1941, he owned the entire company.

A plaque honoring Joe Desimone's contributions to Pike Place Market can be found near the market's entrance.

IN MEMORY OF

GIUSEPPE DESIMONE

WHO, THROUGH HIS DEVOTION AND FORESIGHT, ESTABLISHED POLICIES WHICH GUIDED THE DESTINY OF THE PIKE PLACE MARKET FROM 1926 TO 1946 AND WHICH POLICIES WERE CARRIED FORTH BY HIS FAMILY UNTIL 1974

But back on the farms of South Park, things were changing. The straightening of the Duwamish River between 1913 and 1920 saw the shallow, twisting waterway transformed into a straight, deep commercial channel, destroying more than 97% of the river's wildlife habitat and drawing new industry to the area, including the Boeing Company. The rapid growth Seattle experienced during World War II was felt acutely in South Park, where the tiny community found itself facing a critical housing shortage due to demand from the thousands of newly arrived workers with jobs at Boeing and area shipyards. Industry pressure only continued to mount. The lush lands that had one sprouted carrots, lettuce, and radishes were paved over.

However, not all is lost. Remnants of the town's agricultural roots can still be seen in South Park, now a neighborhood in the city of Seattle. A few such places are highlighted in the pages that follow.

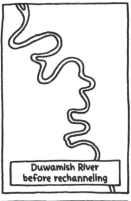

Duwamish River before rechanneling

Duwamish River after rechanneling

Pike Place Market, 1912

Marra-Desimone Park is home to Seattle's only working farm, Marra Farm, an 8.7-acre bastion of beets, berries, and food justice initiatives. The farm is one of only two historical farms within Seattle that maintain an agricultural use today (the other is Wedgwood's Picardo Farm, Seattle's first community garden, famous for being the "P" in Seattle's "P-Patch"). Italian immigrants Carmine and Maria Marra purchased the land in 1920 from Joe Desimone on a handshake, harvesting the land for decades before selling their plot to King County in the 1970s with the promise that its use as farmland be preserved.

Through the work of volunteers, residents, and later, nonprofits and government programs, restoration efforts at the farm began in 1997, with ownership transferred to Seattle Parks and Recreation in 2004. The farm now plays a significant role in the community, just as it did a century ago. In the Giving Garden, hundreds of volunteers work to grow thousands of pounds of fresh organic produce each year to distribute to local food banks, meal programs, and low-income residents across Seattle. Elsewhere on the farm, people come to learn about environmental stewardship, or try their hand at gardening in the P-Patch. Marra Farm is the last working farm in Seattle with a direct link to South Park's agricultural past.

CARMINE AND MARIA MARRA

Solid Ground   Giving Garden

MARRA FARMHOUSE
4th Ave. S.

Around South Park, Carmine and Maria Marra became known as Grandpa and Grandma Marra, with their 1909-built family home well-known among the Italian farmers of the area as a place for warm welcomes and hospitality. Often, Sunday nights were spent enjoying food from Grandma Marra's kitchen and playing a game of cards. The house was owned by the Marra family until the 1980s.

Duwamish Waterway Park is one of only a handful of sites along the Duwamish Waterway that provide the residents of South Park with the ability to gather and sit along the storied river's banks, just as generations did before its rechanneling. Efforts are underway for significant improvements to the park to preserve this slice of history.

DUWAMISH WATERWAY PARK
10th Ave. S.

QUERIO HOUSE
7th Ave. S.

The striking Querio House on 7th Ave. S. was built in 1908, and was owned by local farmer Peter Querio until his death in 1916. Locally known by some South Park residents as the "Witch's Hat House," due to its prominent steep roof, the home received landmark designation in 2004 for its unique design, which reflects both Creole cottage and Indian bungalow influences, the only example of such an architectural style in all of Washington State.

Piper's Orchard

950 NW Carkeek Park Rd. (Carkeek Park)

Stumbling upon the twisting trees of Piper's Orchard in Carkeek Park is like stepping out of time. With over 80 heirloom fruit trees, including 30 that were planted over a century ago, this former family orchard is now a walkable piece of Seattle history and a delight for apple aficionados everywhere.

The story behind Piper's Orchard is nearly as amazing as the orchard itself. It was once the homestead of Andrew Piper and his wife, Wilhelmina, who planted a variety of fruit trees, mostly apples, to sell and use in baking. Years after Andrew Piper's death in 1904, the property was sold to the city for the development of Carkeek Park. For decades, the orchard sat forgotten and overgrown. It was almost hidden for good until a landscape architect traveling through the park in the early 1980s noticed what appeared to be an apple tree among some underbrush. After clearing the area with the help of volunteers, she discovered over 30 heirloom fruit varieties, and Friends of Piper's Orchard was established to restore the orchard, plant more heritage apple varieties, and provide care to the trees and grounds, efforts that continue today.

Visitors to the orchard can see apple varieties including the Northern Spy, Dolgo crabapple, Red Astrachan, and Wolf River, and marvel at this well-preserved slice of Seattle.

Also look out for:

- Duchess of Oldenburg!
- Worden Seckel!
- Chestnut!
- Bietigheimer!
- Swaar!
- Guyot!
- Italian Prune!
- Golden Russet!
- King!
- The ghost of Wilhelmina Piper?!

Seattle's Best Utility Covers

Distinguished guests, it's an honor to be here this evening as host of the 50th Annual Seattle Utility Cover Awards, celebrating the best and brightest of the city's utility cover scene. Often overlooked, the metal beauties beneath us provide access to storm drains, water supplies, and a swath of utilities, some city-owned, some privately owned, some well-known, some long-forgotten. Together, they create a unique patchwork quilt throughout the city. Welcome to the Seattle Utility Cover Awards!

MISS SEWER SEATTLE

Winner of the Rising Star Award

Puget Sound Power & Light Co. ☆ Pine St. between 1st Ave. & Pike Pl.

P. S. P. & L. CO.

This utility cover isn't one to brag, but it has plenty of reason to: it made a brief appearance in the 1993 blockbuster *Sleepless in Seattle*, during the scene where Tom Hanks's character says, "So how's my butt?"

In 1997, the Puget Sound Power and Light Company merged with the Washington Energy Company to become Puget Sound Energy, the utility company Seattleites know and tolerate today.

42

Winners of the Most Dramatic Award

North side of Pike St. between 2nd and 3rd Avenues

Seattle Electric Company

Mutual Light & Heat Co.

These two companies were rivals, so the fact that they've had to spend over 100 years as neighbors may be a form of karmic justice. In an odd tale recounted in the *Seattle Daily Times* in 1905, Mutual Light & Heat was accused of cutting wires that had been installed by the Seattle Electric Company in the Eitel Building (now home to the State Hotel) on the corner of 2nd Ave. and Pike St., just a block away from where these utility covers now sit. What a power struggle! Both companies were short-lived. Mutual Light & Heat was purchased by the Seattle-Tacoma Power Company in 1905 and officially dissolved the following year. The Seattle Electric Company was reincorporated as the Puget Sound Traction, Light & Power Company in 1912.

Winner of the Best Dressed Award

NW 58th St. between 14th and 15th Avenues NW

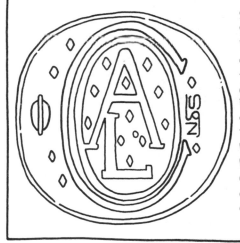

Sitting under a tree outside St. Alphonsus Church in Ballard is a stylish "coal hole," a sidewalk hatch formerly used for the delivery of coal, with an elegant design that incorporates festive diamond shapes with the letters C-O-A-L. The cover was manufactured before the early 1920s by the Niedergesaess & Sons Electric Company, which had a foundry and machine shop at the base of Queen Anne Hill.

Winners of the Lifetime Achievement Award

These styles of utility covers, found throughout the city, have graced Seattle's streets for over 60 years:

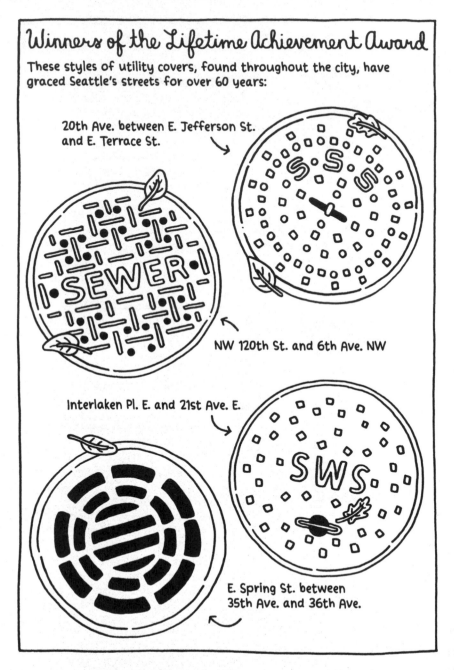

20th Ave. between E. Jefferson St. and E. Terrace St.

NW 120th St. and 6th Ave. NW

Interlaken Pl. E. and 21st Ave. E.

E. Spring St. between 35th Ave. and 36th Ave.

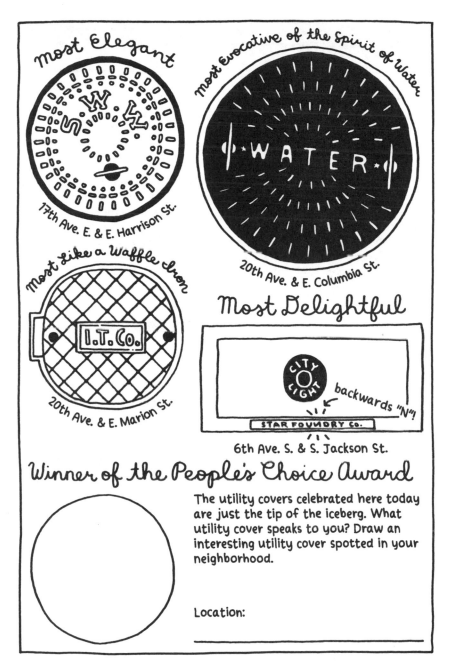

Most Elegant

17th Ave. E. & E. Harrison St.

Most Evocative of the Spirit of Water

WATER

20th Ave. & E. Columbia St.

Most Like a Waffle Iron

I.T.Co.

20th Ave. & E. Marion St.

Most Delightful

CITY LIGHT

backwards "N"!

STAR FOUNDRY Co.

6th Ave. S. & S. Jackson St.

Winner of the People's Choice Award

The utility covers celebrated here today are just the tip of the iceberg. What utility cover speaks to you? Draw an interesting utility cover spotted in your neighborhood.

Location:

HIDDEN GEMS IN A NOT-SO-HIDDEN SPOT

While everyone else is playing volleyball and taking in the views at popular Alki Beach, you can start your own private Seattle Sea Glass Spotters Club and partake in life's greatest solo beach activity: searching for little shimmers of naturally tumbled glass along the shoreline.

For many years, Seattle dumped countless tons of garbage into Elliott Bay, as large bodies of water were seen as a convenient, seemingly infinite answer to the trash problem. Fortunately, discarded jars and bottles can be transformed into treasure. Waves break the glass up and toss the shards in the sand, smoothing them. The result: small bits of sea glass on the beach, which are as pretty as they are collectible. The currents of Puget Sound make Alki Beach during low tide an ideal spot to find sea glass.

EXCLUSIVE OFFER! Your very own Sea Glass Spotters membership card!

Seattle Sea Glass Spotters Club

Name: _____
MEMBER IN GOOD STANDING

Favorite color: _____

Least favorite color: _____

_____
SIGNATURE   EXPIRES: NEVER

cut along dotted line (unless this is a library book!)

draw yourself in box

46

BROUGHT TO YOU BY
ACTIVISM!

El Centro de la Raza	2524 16th Ave. S.

After an English and Adult Basic Education program at South Seattle Community College lost its funding in 1972, activist Roberto Maestas, along with teachers, students, and other community members, occupied  an abandoned elementary school in Beacon Hill with the hopes of converting the building into a community center and a new home for the program that had been cut. Members of the group took turns occupying the building day and night, and despite an unusually cold winter and no heat or running water in the vacant school, they protested peacefully there for about three months until they successfully negotiated with the City of Seattle and the Seattle School District to lease the property. Today, El Centro de la Raza—"The Center for People of All Races"—provides a variety of social and educational services, including legal aid and small business support.

"Ramps to Nowhere" 2300 Arboretum Dr. E.

In the Washington Park Arboretum, there is concrete evidence that development is not always a foregone conclusion. The park is home to remnants of the "Ramps to Nowhere," from an ambitious freeway project that aimed to connect Interstate 90 with the original State Route 520 floating bridge by cutting through the Central District, Madison Valley, and the Arboretum. While Seattle's voters had initially approved the expressway in 1960, by the end of the decade public attitudes were changing as increased awareness of environmental issues and concerns over rising fuel costs led some to rethink a car-centric approach to city life, especially at the cost of displacing people from their communities. Through circulating petitions and blocking bulldozers, a grassroots group of anti-freeway activists successfully pressured the city to reconsider the project. The Seattle City Council voted to remove the would-be R. H. Thomson Expressway from its plans in 1970, with voters overwhelmingly rejecting the project in another ballot measure two years later.

For many decades, the Ramps to Nowhere stood in puzzling contrast to their lush green surroundings. In 2013, the Washington State Department of Transportation announced plans to finally tear down the ramps, but some wanted to see the ramps at least partially preserved as a tribute to citizen activism. As a compromise, in 2016 the city council passed a resolution requesting that a small section of the Ramps to Nowhere be preserved, with the city accepting responsibility for its maintenance.

Daybreak Star Indian Cultural Center
5011 Bernie Whitebear Way (in Discovery Park)

THIS LAND IS OUR LAND

YOU ARE ON INDIAN LAND FORT LAWTON

In the 1960s, Seattle was home to the largest urban Native American population west of Tulsa and north of San Francisco, but there were no funds specifically earmarked for services or programs for Native people. When the federal government announced in 1964 that Magnolia's army post, Fort Lawton, would be downsizing and that about 500 acres of land would be declared surplus, Native activists took notice, eyeing the location for the creation of a much-needed cultural center. At the same time, City of Seattle leadership saw the beautiful mountain views, sandy beaches, and meadows of the property as the ideal setting for a new public park. Several years passed before either group could make a move. While united in their desire for a cultural center, Native activists disagreed about the most effective way to pursue it. Some, inspired by recent Native-led occupation protests at Alcatraz Island in San Francisco Bay, favored similar direct action to achieve their goal, seeking to occupy and reclaim the land based on treaty rights, while others agreed with then-mayor Wes Uhlman, who felt that any negotiations should wait until after the city had officially acquired the land. However, when a press conference announcing plans for the park made no mention of the cultural center or any intention to involve Native Americans in the park development process, activists felt like time was of the essence.

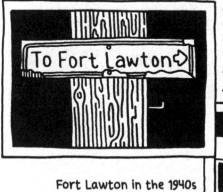

To Fort Lawton ⬭

Fort Lawton in the 1940s

SIGN OF THE TIMES! This wayfinding sign on a utility pole where Gilman Ave. W. meets W. Emerson Pl. in Magnolia is likely over 50 years old.

EAST GATE FORT LAWTON

STOP

On March 8, 1970, a group led by Native activists, including Bernie Whitebear of the Colville Confederated Tribes, arrived at Fort Lawton with the intent of reclaiming the land. However, unbeknownst to the activists, a battalion of military police were on-site at the fort, and protesters were quickly detained. Undeterred, the activists later returned, making several other attempts to occupy the fort before settling in near the entrance with picket signs and a vigil. The unfolding struggle attracted worldwide media attention, helped in part by vocal support from actress and activist Jane Fonda, which ultimately helped sway public opinion and gave activists the opportunity to take their fight from the fort to the bargaining table. The nonprofit United Indians of All Tribes Foundation was established, and after long negotiations, a compromise was reached: 20 acres of what would become known as Discovery Park would go to UIATF for the creation of the Daybreak Star Indian Cultural Center. The center opened its doors in 1977. Bernie Whitebear served as its director until his death in 2000.

I-90 PEDESTRIAN ᴬɴᴅ BIKE TUNNEL

Entrance through Sam Smith Park
1400 MLK Jr. Way S. | Mount Baker

The 1,330-foot-long I-90 pedestrian and bicycle tunnel through Mount Baker Ridge features an assortment of artsy murals that were painted in 1989 and 1990 by a group of Central District teenagers as part of the city's Summer Youth Employment Program, and walking through to admire their work feels like an off-the-beaten-path gallery tour. While many of the murals have been partially painted over through the years, likely due to attempts to cover up graffiti, these touches make for an interesting, strange patchwork of paint and time. As a bonus, during the warm summer months the path's many cyclists breezing past serve as human air conditioners for weary walkers. The tunnel concludes at the East Portal Viewpoint overlooking I-90, Lake Washington, and the Cascade mountains, a delightful scene.

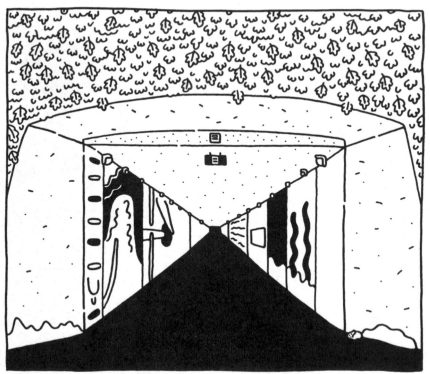

Foot-Friendly Bridges SPANNING THE YEARS

FRINK PARK BRIDGE
398 Lake Washington Blvd. S.

√ Built between 1909 and 1911

√ A concrete gem decorated with a clover pattern

√ In the heart of the park, next to trails leading through a wooded ravine

ARBORETUM AQUEDUCT Lake Washington Blvd. E., near E. Lynn St.

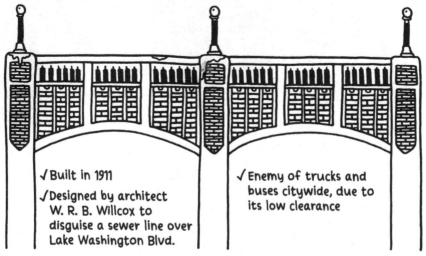

√ Built in 1911

√ Designed by architect W. R. B. Willcox to disguise a sewer line over Lake Washington Blvd.

√ Enemy of trucks and buses citywide, due to its low clearance

RAVENNA PARK BRIDGE 5520 Ravenna Ave. NE

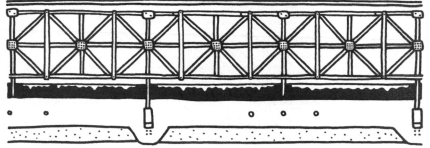

✓ Built in 1913
✓ Designated as both a local and national landmark
✓ The oldest three-hinged steel lattice-arch bridge in Washington State

EAST PINE STREET PEDESTRIAN BRIDGE E. Pine St. & Madrona Dr.

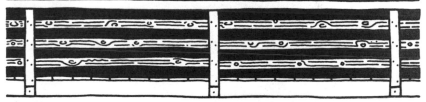

✓ Connects Madrona Dr. and Evergreen Pl.
✓ An unexpected delight in a residential area

SCHMITZ PARK BRIDGE 5551 SW Admiral Way

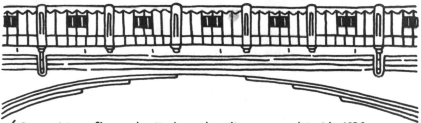

✓ Opened to a fireworks display when it was completed in 1936
✓ Art deco cutie designed by Seattle city engineer Clark Eldridge, who
   also designed the Cowen Park and North Queen Anne Drive Bridges
✓ A designated Seattle landmark since 1980

CARKEEK PARK RAILROAD FOOT BRIDGE
950 NW Carkeek Park Rd.

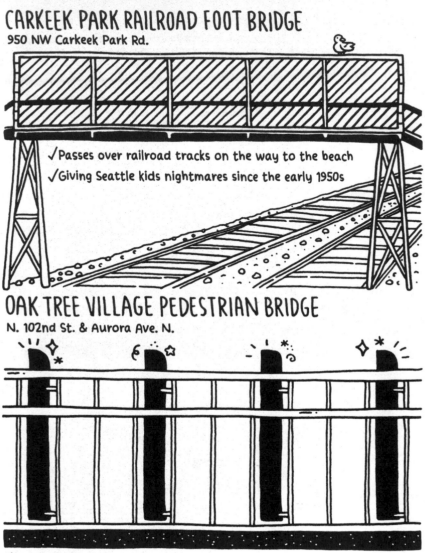

✓Passes over railroad tracks on the way to the beach

✓Giving Seattle kids nightmares since the early 1950s

OAK TREE VILLAGE PEDESTRIAN BRIDGE
N. 102nd St. & Aurora Ave. N.

✓Built in 1961

✓The bridge's *Aurora Bright Dawn* art installation, designed by artist Vicki Scuri, was unveiled in 2019

✓The art installation has hundreds of translucent panels that shimmer in the sun

SALMON BONE BRIDGE
Delridge Way SW & SW Graham St.

✓ Built in the Longfellow Creek
  Natural Area in the early
  2000s

✓ Designed by artist Lorna
  Jordan

AMGEN HELIX PEDESTRIAN BRIDGE
Elliott Ave. W. & W. Prospect St.

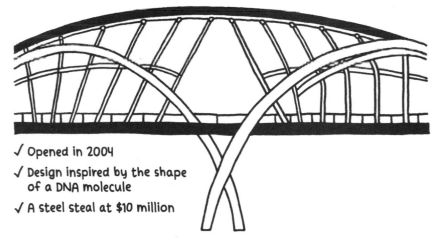

✓ Opened in 2004

✓ Design inspired by the shape
  of a DNA molecule

✓ A steel steal at $10 million

PORT OF SEATTLE
PARKS

HIDDEN GEMS

Most of Seattle's parks are owned and maintained by the Seattle Parks and Recreation department, but these parks are maintained by the Port of Seattle. As such, they aren't as well-known as some of the other parks in the city.

Centennial Park: North of 2711 Alaskan Way

Myrtle Edwards Park's waterfront neighbor is all about the views. You can enjoy sights of Elliott Bay, Mount Rainier, and the Olympic Mountains from the park's flat pedestrian paths.

Bridge Gear Park: Southeast of 3431 11th Ave. SW

This tiny park on Harbor Island features some of the gears from the original Spokane Street Bridge, a 1924 bascule bridge that predated the West Seattle Bridge. The earlier bridge was damaged after being rammed by a freighter ship in 1978. For true bridge fans only!

Terminal 107 Park: 4500 Duwamish Trail

Located in south Elliott Bay along the Duwamish Waterway, this eight-acre park has benches, a walking trail, and art installations that give you a new angle from which to appreciate the city.

Jack Block Park: 2130 Harbor Ave. SW

The most important thing to know about this West Seattle park is that its namesake, Jack Block, longshoreman and Seattle port commissioner from 1973 until 2001, won Carnation Milk's "Baby of the Week" title during the Great Depression. The second-most important thing to know is that this a wonderful park with a shoreline walking path and a 45-foot high observation area with views of the city skyline that rival those from nearby Alki Beach. The park also provides a bird's-eye view of Harbor Island's freight yards and ships.

Downtown & Pioneer Square's
CLUSTER LIGHTS
An Illuminating History

If a Seattleite living in the early 20th century were transported to Seattle today, they would undoubtedly have a lot of questions about their fair city. Yet there is one thing they would almost certainly recognize: Downtown and Pioneer Square's ornamental streetlights, called "cluster lights." If you've been Downtown at any point in the last 100 years, you've probably seen these towering treasures, whether or not you've taken a moment to reflect on their charming presence. With ornate bases and globe-shaped festive light covers, this style of streetlight has been lining Seattle's busiest thoroughfares for over a century.

The idea for the city's cluster lights dates back to the 1900s, when Seattle had a mission: to become the

"best lighted city in America"

ahead of the Alaska-Yukon-Pacific Exposition, Seattle's first world's fair. While Seattle had had hanging streetlights installed in 1905, more permanent cluster lights were seen as an inexpensive improvement. To reach their goal would mean streetlights—lots of them—taking full advantage of all the new, modern electricity options now available.

Buzz over a plan to install streetlights along 1st, 2nd, and 3rd Avenues began in 1906, but it wouldn't be until January 1909 that 3rd Ave.'s 117 cluster lights were first illuminated. The demand for more was immediate. Within weeks, petitions and permits were flying from business owners across the city eager to see the lights on their own blocks.

"Petitions are in circulation which contemplate the installation of cluster lights on Union Street from Second Avenue to Hubbell Way and Pike Street, and also on Pine Street from First Avenue to Broadway. Pike Street and Westlake are expected to follow,"

Seattle civic leader Henry Broderick reported in February 1909.

"These, with the illumination already ordered on First, Second, Third and Fourth Avenues, will create a continuous brilliance of nearly eight miles and will form a night promenade for visitors unequaled in this country."

The lights quickly became a selling point to Downtown living.

"EVERYBODY is trying to get on to 3rd Ave. now to enjoy the CLUSTER LIGHTS. Don't blame them,"

read an apartment ad from that same month.

Soon, Seattle's "best lighted" ambitions were realized. Directory publisher R. L. Polk, visiting in June 1909 to get an early look at exposition preparations, called Seattle "one of the handsomest cities in the entire country" and remarked that the cluster lights along 1st, 2nd, and 3rd Avenues "give the whole section an appearance of splendor difficult to describe."

"Seattle has a lot of things we want down in Atlanta," Atlanta mayor R. F. Maddox reflected after visiting in September 1909, "and cluster lights is one."

A year later, "the cluster light fad" as the *Seattle Daily Times* called it, had

"reached every section of the city, including Capitol Hill, Pike and Pine Streets, the entire Denny Hill and Jackson Street regrade districts and Western Avenue, in addition to all crosstown streets in the business district."

The lights continued to be the talk of the town in the years that followed.

"The attractive street lights of the metropolis of the Pacific Northwest have been a source of wonder and admiration to visitors ever since the cluster system was installed,"

the *Seattle Daily Times* wrote in 1912. At a meeting to discuss the merits of various types of street lighting the same year, electrical engineer S. C. Lindsay remarked,

"I think Seattle has the finest example of street illumination from posts and cluster lights that there is in this country. I have not seen the cluster lights in all other cities, but have seen three or four other examples, and do not see how it is possible to improve on the Seattle cluster lights. I will go further and say the cluster lamps in Portland are not one-third as good."

DAAAANG!
Sick burn!

Over the years, the poles have continued to be maintained and refurbished as needed. In 2019, Seattle City Light worked to convert all the remaining cluster lights to more energy-efficient LED fixtures. While most of Seattle's remaining historic streetlights are concentrated in Downtown and Pioneer Square, you can find a few outliers, like outside the Park Lane apartment building, at 400 Boylston Ave. E. on Capitol Hill, and outside the old Georgetown City Hall. One of the nicest sets of cluster lights can be found on the Pike Street Hill Climb between Alaskan Way and Western Ave. below Pike Place Market. There, several cluster lights with five light globes each dot the walking path.

Two types of bases:

Olympic Foundry won the contract to provide many of the streetlamps' iron posts. Posts with the company's emblem on the bottom can be still be found today, like this one near Rainier Playfield in the Columbia City neighborhood.

OLYMPIC
FOUNDRY
SEATTLE

CITY OF SEATTLE
1869

This more ornate base features the City of Seattle's old seal.

ELL STREET PIE

| Pier 66, 2225 Alaskan Way | The Waterfront |

You can't beat the sights of Puget Sound from the rooftop deck at Bell Street Pier. This deck has the rare combination of being in the heart of Seattle while also managing to remain fairly quiet and free from crowds, and it offers fantastic views of the Seattle waterfront from plenty of tables and benches, perfect for catching a moment of relaxation.

The Bell Street Pier deck is not the first rooftop park in this location, however. According to the book *The Seattle Waterfront: An Illustrated History* by Paul Dorpat, the original public rooftop park at what is now Pier 66 opened in 1915 and was outfitted with benches, plants, and a solarium, as well as Happy Land, a day care of sorts, where children could be watched while their parents shopped nearby. Five short years later, the rooftop park was closed; it was considered to be a "moral nuisance," with a reputation as a spot more popular with sailors and their companions than with children and their families. It wouldn't open again to the public until 1998, this time as the Bell Street Pier rooftop deck (now with fewer moral nuisances!).

Mount Rainier from the pier ⤵

Secrets of Popular Parks & Playfields

Golden Gardens Park

8498 Seaview Pl. NW (Ballard)

The enduring tradition of fire pits on the beach at Golden Gardens began in 1962 at the suggestion of a citizen.

THANKS, CITIZEN!

Hiawatha Playfield

2700 California Ave. SW (West Seattle)

HIAWATHA COMMUNITY CENTER

← built in 1911

← first public recreation building in Seattle

← oldest community center west of the Mississippi

Gas Works Park

← The site of the Seattle Gas Light Company from 1906 until 1956

2101 N. Northlake Way (Wallingford)

The concrete arches near the entrance to the park are the remnants of train trestles for coal cars that once made deliveries to the gas plant.

Volunteer Park

1247 15th Ave. E. (Capitol Hill)

Near the 14th Ave. entrance to the park, south of the water tower

Gift from Victoria, BC, in 1965 →

This 1937 lamp once stood outside British Columbia's Parliament Buildings.

Washington Park Arboretum

1075 Lake Washington Blvd. E. (Montlake)

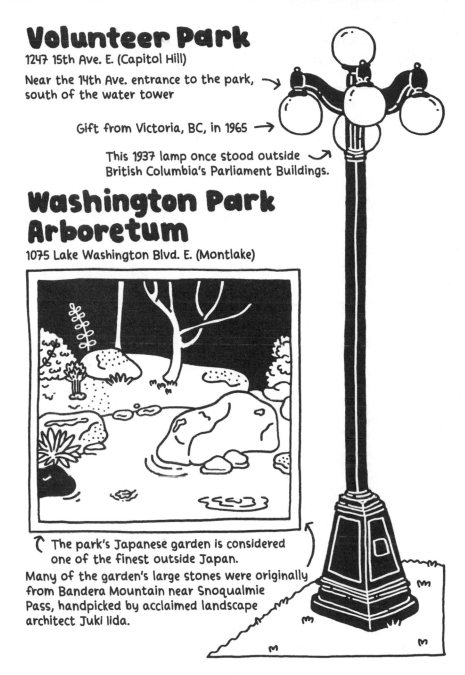

The park's Japanese garden is considered one of the finest outside Japan.

Many of the garden's large stones were originally from Bandera Mountain near Snoqualmie Pass, handpicked by acclaimed landscape architect Juki Iida.

Woodland Park Rose Garden

750 N. 50th St. (Green Lake)

sculpture installed in 1924

created by Alice Carr, the
first woman to recieve
a public sculpture commission
in Seattle ↘

Cascade Playground & P-Patch

333 Pontius Ave. N. (Cascade/South Lake Union)
The closest park to the center of Seattle!

A plaque, located on Minor Ave. N. between
← Harrison and Thomas Streets, across from
the park, marks the geographical center
point of the city.

Lincoln Park

8011 Fauntleroy Way SW (West Seattle)

Workers of the Civil Works
Administration and Works
Progress Administration programs
of the 1930s helped add
infrastructure to Lincoln Park,
including trails and a seawall. A
WPA stamp can be seen on parts
of the concrete seawall in the park.

Alki Beach Park
2665 Alki Ave. SW (West Seattle)

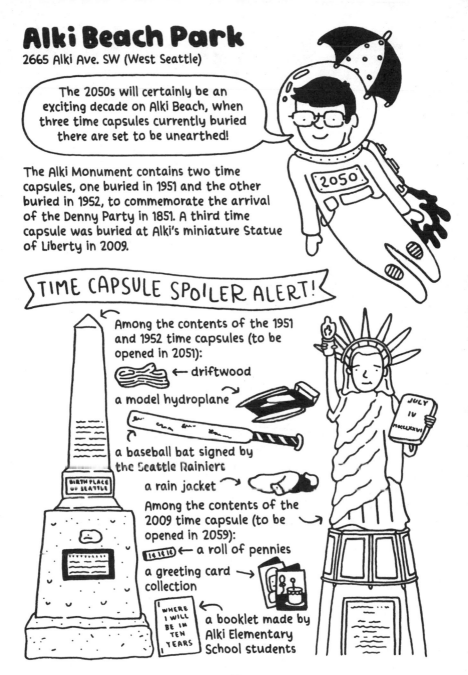

The 2050s will certainly be an exciting decade on Alki Beach, when three time capsules currently buried there are set to be unearthed!

The Alki Monument contains two time capsules, one buried in 1951 and the other buried in 1952, to commemorate the arrival of the Denny Party in 1851. A third time capsule was buried at Alki's miniature Statue of Liberty in 2009.

TIME CAPSULE SPOILER ALERT!

Among the contents of the 1951 and 1952 time capsules (to be opened in 2051):

← driftwood

a model hydroplane

a baseball bat signed by the Seattle Rainiers

a rain jacket →

Among the contents of the 2009 time capsule (to be opened in 2059):

← a roll of pennies

a greeting card collection →

a booklet made by Alki Elementary School students

BIRTH PLACE OF SEATTLE

WHERE I WILL BE IN TEN YEARS

JULY IV MDCCLXXVI

The Queen Anne neighborhood is Seattle public stairway royalty, with over 100 city-maintained staircases, but other areas have steps worthy of a crown. The following stairs were selected for their ability to be easily incorporated into a longer walk. Enjoy the climb!

Dose Terrace Stairs: S. Dose Terrace from Lake Washington Blvd. S. to 34th Ave. S.
Stair count: 138

These ornate, gorgeous stairs overlooking Lake Washington are worthy of a visit in their own right, so the fact that they happen to be in the middle of so many other great things to see is the cherry on top! Enjoy getting up close and personal with the lake, or check out nearby historic Colman Park. For a more ambitious walk, head to Bradner Gardens Park (page 20) before visiting Sam Smith Park and the I-90 bicycle tunnel (page 52), or take in an unexpected view of Downtown Seattle from the Mount Baker Ridge Viewpoint. WALK POTENTIAL: EXTREME!

Thistle Street Stairs: SW Thistle St. from Northrop Pl. SW to 46th Ave. SW
Stair count: 367

The Thistle Street Stairs are the second-longest public stairway in Seattle, after Capitol Hill's Howe Street Stairs. After descending the steps, stop for a quick visit at nearby Solstice Park, spend a day exploring Lincoln Park's many trails, or watch the ferries come and go from the Fauntleroy Ferry Terminal.

52nd Street Stairs: Access through the Ravenna P-Patch Community Garden at Ravenna Ave. NE and NE 52nd St.
Stair count: 218

From the stairs, walk to Ravenna Park and find the delightful Ravenna Park Bridge from 1913, or go on a longer trek, toward the University of Washington campus, to check out Sylvan Theater or the Medicinal Herb Garden (pages 34 and 35).

FLOATING HOMES of LAKE UNION

Seattle's buoyant and beloved houseboat scene wasn't always centered on Lake Union. By the time a ship canal project connected Lake Washington and Puget Sound—with a stop at Lake Union along the way—an eclectic mix of houseboats had dotted the city's bodies of water for years. In the early 1900s, the scrappy shacks built on barges in Elliott Bay that some of the city's laborers called home were only a cable car ride away from the fancy houseboat community that had sprung up on Lake Washington near affluent Madison Park, popular with well-to-do Seattleites as summer homes.

"Of all the forms of summer outdoor life, houseboating combines the maximum of comfort with a minimum of the annoyances that sometimes accompany life away from one's convenient city home," wrote the *Seattle Daily Times* in 1905. "Seattle people, although they have no legitimate excuse for leaving town in summer as people who live in hot cities have, nevertheless prefer to spice their lives with that variety which keeps existence from becoming flat, and so they build houseboats and go to the lake and various points on the Sound to live on the water that they can see from almost every street in town."

Not everyone was thrilled with these communities. A year later, the newspaper reported the complaints of property owners along Lake Washington, who "asked that something be done to regulate the alleged evils resulting from houseboats" on the lake, saying that "refuse of all kinds is constantly being thrown from the houseboats into the water... rendering the shore in places offensive," and that "campers on the shore are also said to be a nuisance in this respect."

Similar complaints would dog Seattle's houseboat owners for decades to come. It would take a long time, a lot of activism and community organizing, and perhaps a Tom Hanks-Meg Ryan blockbuster, for houseboats to earn the sort of legitimacy they see today. Walking the Cheshiahud Lake Union Loop is a great way to catch a glimpse of today's floating homes, which are no longer seen as a blight, but as a celebrated part of Seattle's cityscape.

W--NE- H--"E -- T

Niceee!

- Docked on the northwest portion of Lake Union, near the base of the Aurora Bridge
- Built before 1912
- Originally on Lake Washington
- One of Seattle's few remaining intact, early floating homes
- Formerly owned by Dick and Colleen Wagner, who established the Center for Wooden Boats out of their houseboat

The Center for Wooden Boats is now in Lake Union Park on the south side of the lake.

"SLEEPLESS HOUSEBOAT"

- On the west side of Lake Union
- Built in 1978
- Made a splash when featured in the 1993 blockbuster *Sleepless in Seattle*

GET TO KNOW a HOUSEBOAT RESIDENT

Of all the colorful characters who have called Seattle home, few have reached Robert W. Patten's level of notoriety. Known as "the Umbrella Man," Patten was an early Lake Union houseboat dweller whose tall tales about his life were as compelling as the self-made umbrella hat he sported around town. Patten did odd jobs, sold "a glue of his own mixing," according to the *Seattle Daily Times*, and claimed to have been close friends with Abraham Lincoln. Already prominent enough that "practically all Seattle came to know him by sight," Patten's fame rose even higher when his depiction was used in the newspaper's daily weather reports, Illustrated by cartoonist John "Dok" Hager, alongside a duck named the Kid. When Patten suffered a stroke in 1910, the event was front-page news. He died in 1913.

TINY PARKS, BIG VIEWS!

HIDDEN GEMS

Less than an acre each!

Weather Watch Park: 4035 Beach Dr. SW

On a clear day, you can enjoy views of the islands and the Olympic Mountains from this park, built where a popular dock once stood.

51st Avenue NE Street End: 51st Ave. NE and NE Laurelcrest Ln.

Offering a multimillion-dollar view for the low, low cost of absolutely nothing, this shoreline street end with a picnic table is a great spot to eat a snack while you admire Mount Rainier in the distance.

Fremont Peak Park: 4357 Palatine Ave. N.

There's a lot to enjoy at this park on a promontory, whether it's the cute conifer trees, the neat public art, or the views of Puget Sound and the ship canal.

Terry Pettus Park: 2001 Fairview Ave. E.

With sweeping lakeside views, this park along Lake Union is a fitting tribute to its namesake. Terry Pettus, a union organizer, activist, and reporter, was instrumental in saving Lake Union's houseboats in the 1970s.

DEEP ROOTS

Trees of Seattle

The rich greenery of Seattle has persuaded countless people to call the Emerald City their home. Of course, the allure wasn't always the prospect of actually keeping the trees alive: Seattle's earliest fortunes were due in large part to the town's burgeoning timber industry, which over many years irrevocably transformed the forested land where the Duwamish people had lived and worked for thousands of years into the city we know today.

Thankfully, Seattle is still a city of great trees and great stories, and taking a moment to appreciate their unique beauty and variety is a gift that keeps on giving. In this section, we'll get to know some trees that are worth a second look (though, sometimes the most extraordinary trees are ones that mysteriously call your name from across the street, for reasons unknown).

JAPANESE MAPLES

Kubota Garden
9817 55th Ave. S.

With waterfalls, sculptures, tucked-away bridges, and scenic overlooks, Kubota Garden is the stunner of South Seattle. The garden is also remarkable for its many varieties of Japanese maples, which burst into a kaleidoscope of color in the fall.

INTERLAKEN PARK 2451 DELMAR DR. E.

Quietly nestled between Capitol Hill and Montlake, Interlaken Park could be considered a hidden gem, as sometimes the bird sightings outpace the number of people you'll pass while traversing the park's winding paths. Among a grove of coast redwood trees, one awe-inspiring specimen stands above them all at nearly 200 feet, making it the tallest of its kind in the state. You're likely to spot it without seeking it out.

DAWN REDWOODS

Carl S. English Jr. Botanical Garden 🔔 3015 NW 54th St.

This seven-acre garden at Ballard's Hiram M. Chittenden Locks was lovingly cultivated over many decades by the head gardener for whom the park would go on to be named, a man whose passion for botany was matched by his green thumb and grand visions.

Millions of years ago, the dawn redwood was one of the most common tree species in the Northern Hemisphere. It was thought to be completely extinct until the 1940s, when an enormous dawn redwood was discovered in a remote valley of China's Sichuan province. Seeds from the tree were collected in 1948 and distributed to dozens of institutions by Harvard University's Arnold Arboretum. Carl English was the lucky recipient of some of the coveted seeds, and planted them in the garden, making him among the first in the country to reintroduce the dawn redwood to Seattle landscapes.

CARL S. ENGLISH JR.

GARRY OAKS

Seward Park 🌰 5900 Lake Washington Blvd. S.

Seward Park is perhaps Seattle's most delightful destination for tree lovers, with no shortage of fantastic foliage, including some of the city's few remaining old-growth trees, and wonderful Douglas firs that will give you a new appreciation for the classic conifer. The Garry oak holds the distinguished title as the only oak species native to Washington State, but it has seen its population dwindle in recent years due to development and invasive species. However, a few can be seen around Seward Park, including one on the south shore of the peninsula, accessible by walking east, past the parking lot, until you enter an open prairie.

SEATTLE TREE TALES

One of Seattle's wildest tree sagas has roots on the University of Washington campus, near the unassuming intersection of Pend Oreille Rd. NE and E. Stevens Way. The story begins in 1896, when a UW graduate student studying at Harvard became smitten with a majestic elm growing at nearby Cambridge Common, which boasted a most illustrious backstory. It was said that it was under that tree's lush, green canopy that General George Washington had taken command of the Continental Army in the Revolutionary War on July 3, 1775, forever changing the course of American history. The student felt that growing an offspring of the tree on the campus of his alma mater would be a great way to honor the man for whom Washington State had been named. After successfully growing a sapling from cuttings of the "Washington elm," the student sent it by express mail to UW professor Edmond Meany in 1902, with a letter stating his hope that it would grace the campus for the next 200 years. It was planted shortly thereafter, and it thrived.

The original tree in Massachusetts wouldn't fare as well. In 1923, the 200-year-old tree from which the UW tree had descended was diseased and fragile, with many blaming its demise on improper care and neglect. After it died, UW gardeners carefully cultivated a cutting of their own Washington elm to give back to Cambridge. Additional cuttings were used to grow trees in Olympia, the Washington Park Arboretum, and outside UW's Bagley Hall.

SCION OF THE
WASHINGTON ELM

In the summer of 1963, lightning struck the UW's original Washington elm, and despite efforts to revive it, the tree was removed at the end of 1966. Students of Garfield High School's woodworking class turned a log from the historic tree into six gavels, which were presented to the University of Washington Alumni Association, Western Washington State College, and their own student body, among others. Luckily, in the elm that had been growing outside Bagley Hall for decades, the university had a suitable replacement for their lost landmark tree. The surviving tree was moved to its new home between Clark Hall and the Communications Building in 1967—192 years to the day since George Washington's oath—and was given a plaque to declare its important place in US history.

Then in 2016, despite decades of diligence, UW Grounds Management discovered that the second tree had split, posing a potential safety hazard. Once again, a Washington elm had to be removed completely. In what by then was a long tradition of tree replacement, efforts began to use cuttings from another descendant, the one in the Arboretum, to cultivate a sapling and start anew where the elm once stood. But for now, the 1967 plaque is the only thing that remains of the legendary tree.

The story doesn't end there, however. It turns out that over 100 years of adulation, careful cultivation, patriotic plaques, and joyful teenage gavel-making may be entirely misplaced. According to the Cambridge Historical Commission, there is no definitive proof that George Washington actually took his famous oath under an elm tree in Cambridge Common.

Llandover Woods Greenspace

14499 3rd Ave. NW	Broadview

This quiet haven for all seasons is one of Northwest Seattle's best-kept secrets. In summer, bird-watching and blackberry-picking opportunities abound, while fall and winter bring crunchy leaves and a sense of stillness you'll be hard-pressed to find elsewhere in the city.

During Hollywood's golden age, the center of the film industry in the Pacific Northwest was Seattle's Belltown neighborhood, where an influx of movie-related businesses, theaters, and restaurants earned the once-sleepy stretch of streets the moniker Film Row. It was here that the slightly less glamorous side of show business happened. Major studios, including Warner Brothers, Paramount, and 20th Century Fox, had film exchanges in the neighborhood. These were distribution centers, where film reels were received direct from Los Angeles to be doled out to the hundreds of movie theaters across the northwestern United States, including Alaska. The exchanges also provided space for theater owners and film salespeople to preview movies and talk business. In the 1930s and 1940s, the *Seattle Daily Times* breathlessly covered Film Row comings and goings of even the most minor players in the movie scene, including theater candy promoters.

As technology and transportation changed, so too did Film Row. By the 1960s, the number of studios in the area had dwindled. Universal Studios was the last to leave in 1980. However, a quick walk around Belltown reveals the forgotten stars of Film Row, the buildings that made a little piece of movie magic happen for a generation of theatergoers.

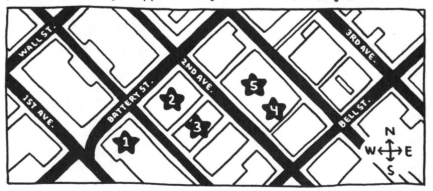

PARAMOUNT FILM EXCHANGE

2300 1st Ave.

The Paramount film exchange, built in 1937, was the studio's distribution center for theaters across the region. Its time in Seattle ended in 1951, when construction of the Battery Street Tunnel required boring through the building's basement.

MGM FILM EXCHANGE

2331 2nd Ave.

Movie studio Metro-Goldwyn-Mayer was the largest in the world during the years that it ran regional distribution out of its Seattle film exchange, boasting contracts with Hollywood superstars like Katharine Hepburn and Clark Gable. The art deco building operated as an exchange from 1936 into the 1950s, during which time reels for films like *The Wizard of Oz* passed through its doors.

3 Lorraine Hotel

2327 2nd Ave.

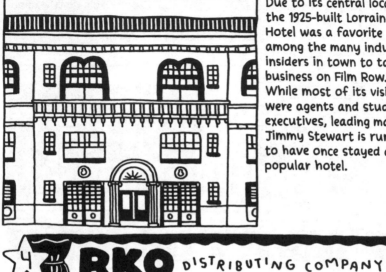

Due to its central location, the 1925-built Lorraine Hotel was a favorite among the many industry insiders in town to talk business on Film Row. While most of its visitors were agents and studio executives, leading man Jimmy Stewart is rumored to have once stayed at the popular hotel.

4 RKO DISTRIBUTING COMPANY

2312 2nd Ave.

The RKO Distributing Company ran its local offices out of this unsung hero of Seattle architecture built in 1928. RKO was the studio behind big movies of the day like 1933's *King Kong* and the distributor of Disney animated films like 1937's *Snow White and the Seven Dwarfs*. Looking closely at the building's exterior reveals beautifully crafted tiles adorned with dragons, ships, and flowers, architectural touches not often seen in Seattle.

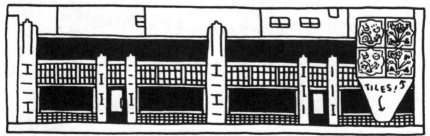

TILES!

2322 2nd Ave.

Across the street from the Lorraine Hotel, the Rendezvous Cafe and Jewel Box Theater became THE gathering place for executives and others in the film industry. The building was originally constructed in 1925 for B. F. Shearer, an extremely successful theatrical supply company, which would go on to provide fixtures like curtains and seats to the 5th Avenue Theatre, the Embassy Theatre (now the Triple Door), and the Paramount Theatre. The Rendezvous was a popular destination on Film Row from the start, and with the addition of the Jewel Box Theater in 1932 for private screenings, film industry folks could have dinner and a movie a stone's throw away from their hotel.

Belltown Cottage Park

2512 Elliott Ave.	Belltown

Sitting among the many restaurants, office buildings, and shiny high-rises of Belltown, the three small cottages on the corner of Elliott Ave. and Vine St. certainly stand out. Surrounded by cheerful murals, tiled mosaic art, and a P-Patch, it's nothing short of amazing that the cottages have managed to survive through all the changes Seattle has seen since they were built over a century ago. At that time, Belltown, known as the Denny Regrade, was a blue-collar neighborhood favored by waterfront workers, and houses like these were a common sight in the community.

The cottages' survival is due in no small part to the dedication of former residents and their friends, who pushed to create a community garden on the land and to protect the cottages from development, eventually winning a landmark designation for the houses in 2000. Now, they live as a symbol of Belltown's past while the adjacent P-Patch invites curious walkers in with its public art and vegetable plots.

☆SEATTLE☆STAR☆SIGNS☆

The signs of Pike Place Market may be some of Seattle's best-known neon icons, but in neighborhoods across the city, there are other signs worth celebrating. Neon signs reached their peak of popularity in the United States between about 1920 and 1960, when cheaper, less labor-intensive methods became available. Now, they are shining examples of a different era of advertising, artistry, and the city.

SW Avalon Way

THE Shack

La-HACIENDA MOTEL

Vacancy

S. Lucile St.

61st Ave. SW

alki HOMESTEAD

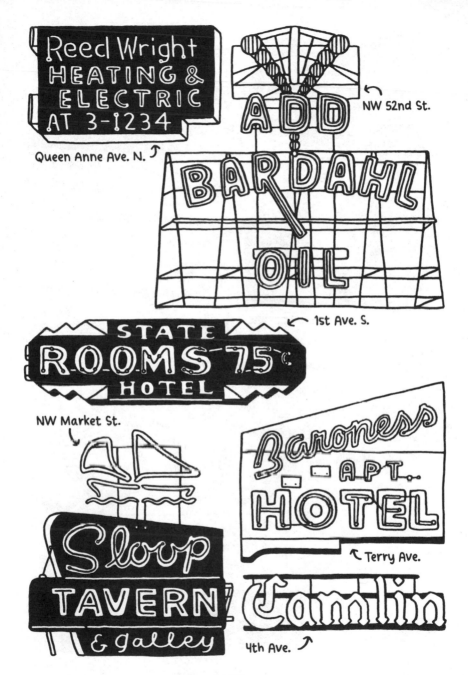

Reed Wright HEATING & ELECTRIC AT 3-1234

Queen Anne Ave. N.

ADD

NW 52nd St.

BARDAHL OIL

1st Ave. S.

STATE ROOMS 75¢ HOTEL

NW Market St.

Baroness APT HOTEL

Terry Ave.

Sloop TAVERN & galley

Camlin

4th Ave.

SW Avalon Way

AVALON

Fiddler's INN

35th Ave. NE

15th Ave. NW

Mac's AUTO TOPS SEAT COVERS

Puetz

Aurora Ave. N.

GOLF

N. 45th St.

SUN CLEANERS

NOMINEES FOR FUTURE NEON Classics

TOP POT DOUGHNUTS

5th Ave.

BUY SELL TRADE USED BOOKS

Harvard Ave.

Broadway E.

HIGH LINE

5 SPOT

Queen Anne Ave. N.

S. Vale St.

GEORGETOWN Records

Wildwood Station Bus Shelter

| S. Wildwood Ln. & Rainier Ave. S. | Rainier Valley |

HIDDEN GEMS

Among the many bus shelters along busy Rainier Ave. stands one that is not like the others. This quaint brick shelter, known as the Wildwood Station shelter, has been serving Seattle's transit commuters for over 100 years, first as a stop along a railway line and later in its current role as bus stop. A short pedestrian trail accessible through the shelter makes a quick connection to Seward Park Ave. S. In a city of nearly 1,800 bus shelters, the Wildwood Station shelter is one of a kind.

SHEDDING LIGHT ON PIONEER SQUARE'S
S I D E W A L K   P R I S M S

In the City of Seattle's early days, Pioneer Square had a problem: having been built on Puget Sound's muddy tidal flatlands, the area flooded with each rising tide, causing the city's primitive sewer system to back up into the streets.

This **STINKS!**
Ha... Ha... Ha...

Just when citizens thought things couldn't get any crappier (sorry, Mom!), on June 6, 1889, a massive fire ripped through Seattle. By the time the final flame was extinguished, over 25 city blocks, most of the city's downtown core, had been reduced to rubble.

Undeterred, Seattle worked quickly to rebuild—bigger, better, and safer than ever. With the post-fire reconstruction boom, city planners found their opportunity to solve the flooding problem once and for all. Streets would be raised one or two stories to be above sea level, a move that would simultaneously prevent future flooding and provide room for the installation of a more modern sewer system. This meant that what was once a building's entrance would now be underground, and storefronts needed to move up a floor or two if they wanted to be at the new street level. Today, the purple-hued glass circles and squares that pepper the sidewalks are small remnants from these big changes. Called "sidewalk prisms" or "vault lights," they allowed sunlight to shine into the underground passageways that the street-raising project had created. Pioneer Square has more intact prism lights than any other neighborhood in Seattle.

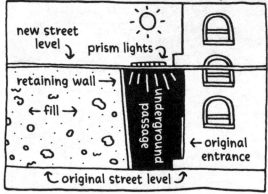

new street level
prism lights
retaining wall →
← fill →
underground passage
← original entrance
⌐ original street level ⌐

While many have been damaged, repaired, or replaced over the years, they represent an impressive engineering feat and serve as a reminder of the underground that lurks beneath the city's streets. On the following pages are just a few notable examples.

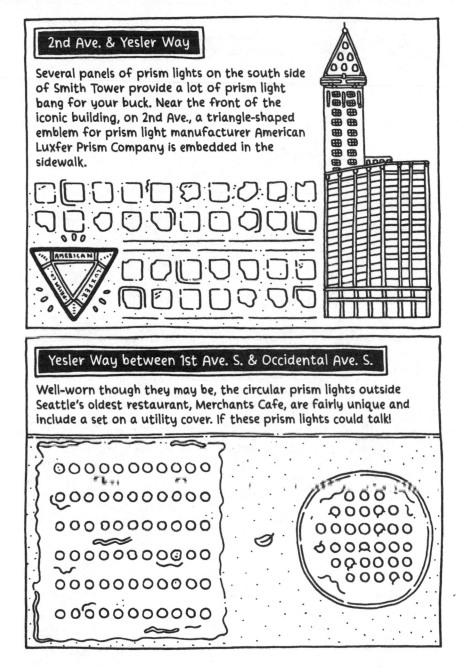

2nd Ave. & Yesler Way

Several panels of prism lights on the south side of Smith Tower provide a lot of prism light bang for your buck. Near the front of the iconic building, on 2nd Ave., a triangle-shaped emblem for prism light manufacturer American Luxfer Prism Company is embedded in the sidewalk.

Yesler Way between 1st Ave. S. & Occidental Ave. S.

Well-worn though they may be, the circular prism lights outside Seattle's oldest restaurant, Merchants Cafe, are fairly unique and include a set on a utility cover. If these prism lights could talk!

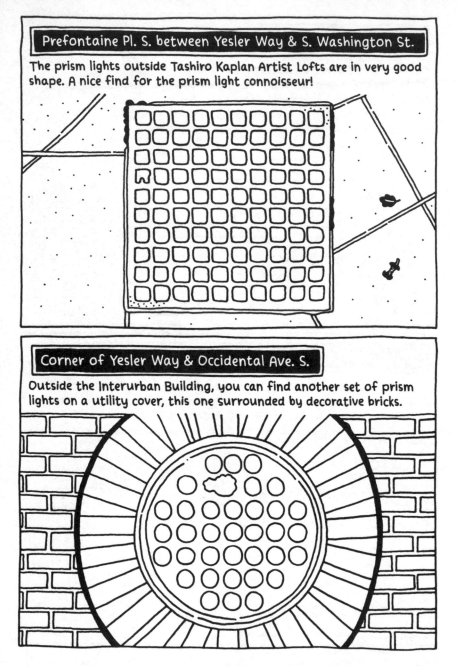

Prefontaine Pl. S. between Yesler Way & S. Washington St.

The prism lights outside Tashiro Kaplan Artist Lofts are in very good shape. A nice find for the prism light connoisseur!

Corner of Yesler Way & Occidental Ave. S.

Outside the Interurban Building, you can find another set of prism lights on a utility cover, this one surrounded by decorative bricks.

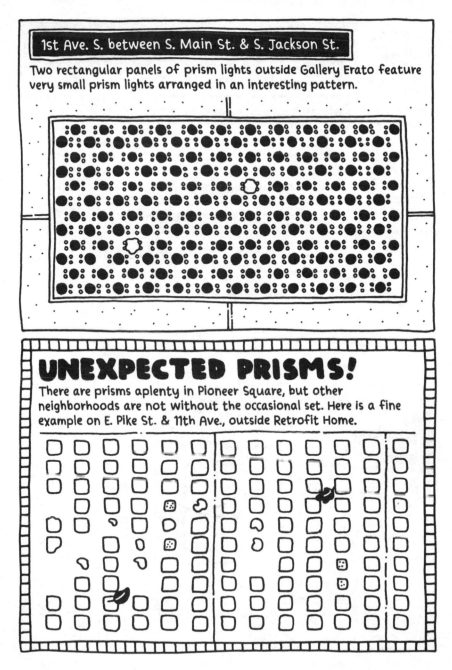

1st Ave. S. between S. Main St. & S. Jackson St.

Two rectangular panels of prism lights outside Gallery Erato feature very small prism lights arranged in an interesting pattern.

UNEXPECTED PRISMS!

There are prisms aplenty in Pioneer Square, but other neighborhoods are not without the occasional set. Here is a fine example on E. Pike St. & 11th Ave., outside Retrofit Home.

Kobe Terrace Park

650 S. Main St. | Chinatown-International District

HIDDEN GEMS

This peaceful hideaway is especially dazzling in the early spring, when the cherry blossoms are in full bloom. The small park is named after Kobe, Japan, one of Seattle's sister cities, which gifted both the beautiful trees and the park's 8,000-pound stone Japanese lantern centerpiece in 1976. A path in the park leads to the the Danny Woo Community Garden, an exceptional gathering place for residents of the neighborhood. It is home to well-cultivated plots, an outdoor kitchen, a fruit orchard, and Seattle's only community-garden chickens.

The Danny Woo Community Garden

Non-Building Landmarks

Since 1973, Seattle has designated more than 450 historical landmarks. While the majority of the city's landmarks are buildings, a handful are objects with interesting histories all their own.

CHINESE COMMUNITY BULLETIN BOARD   DESIGNATED 1976

From building railroads to digging the Montlake Cut, the Chinese laborers who began immigrating to Seattle in the mid-1800s were an essential part of the city's early development. They were accepted at first by other settlers eager to see the city grow, but later in the century racist anti-Chinese sentiment, both locally and nationally, had led to mistrust, exclusionary laws, and violence. And in February 1886, the majority of Seattle's Chinese residents were forcibly expelled from the city that they had helped build.

For the few who remained, the use of community bulletin boards—like the one on the side of the Louisa Hotel, at the corner of S. King St. and 7th Ave. S.—began in the 1890s and became an essential way to share and read news, current events, and messages in Chinese, especially vital for those who read no English. While this particular bulletin board was installed in the 1960s, it was designated a landmark in 1976 because it reflects a long tradition in the area.

Brill Trolley Bus 798 designated 1978

In the late 1930s, Seattle's streetcar and cable car systems were debt-ridden and out-of-date, but voters fresh out of the Great Depression were reluctant to embrace plans for their replacement. After Seattle mayor Arthur B. Langlie secured a federal loan to relieve street railway debt in May of 1939, a fleet of new trackless trolleys were ordered, including 100 to be built locally by the Pacific Car and Foundry Company in Renton.

The investment paid off. Gas rationing during World War II, along with war production jobs bringing more workers to the area, caused ridership to surge, restoring Seattleites' faith in their beleaguered transit system. This Brill trolley bus, made by Pacific Car and Foundry, became a landmark in 1978 for its important role in Seattle's transit history and its adorable art deco paint job. While the bus's rush hour days are behind it, the old trolley is in good hands with the Metro Employees Historic Vehicle Association, a volunteer group dedicated to preserving transportation history in Seattle and King County.

Street clocks rose in popularity across the United States in the early 20th century, but nowhere were they more beloved than in Seattle, where the abundance of cast-iron clocks that dotted the city's streets led many to refer to Seattle as the City of Clocks. In addition to being a practical way for pedestrians to tell the time, the ornate clocks also proved to be effective advertisements for the businesses that displayed them. But time marches on, and by the 1950s, street clocks had fallen out of fashion. Viewing them as nothing more than obsolete sidewalk impediments, the City of Seattle made plans for their removal, causing pushback from clock owners and lovers alike. As a compromise, an ordinance was enacted that required the clocks to either show the correct time or get the boot, which still led to the removal of many of the city's historic timepieces. Despite this, Seattle is still considered to have one of the largest collections of cast-iron street clocks in the United States, and in 1981 a group of nine remaining clocks achieved landmark status together.

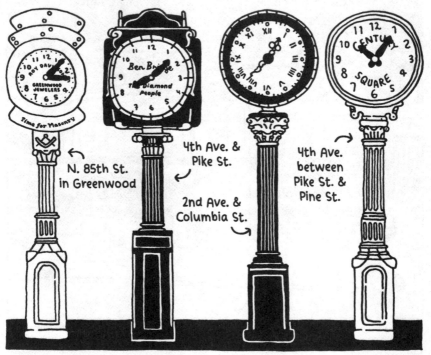

N. 85th St. in Greenwood

4th Ave. & Pike St.

2nd Ave. & Columbia St.

4th Ave. between Pike St. & Pine St.

Lightship No. 83

Lake Union ☆ designated 1989

A.K.A. A FLOATING LIGHTHOUSE!

Built in 1904, this landmark vessel is the oldest steam-driven lightship on the West Coast. It served until 1960.

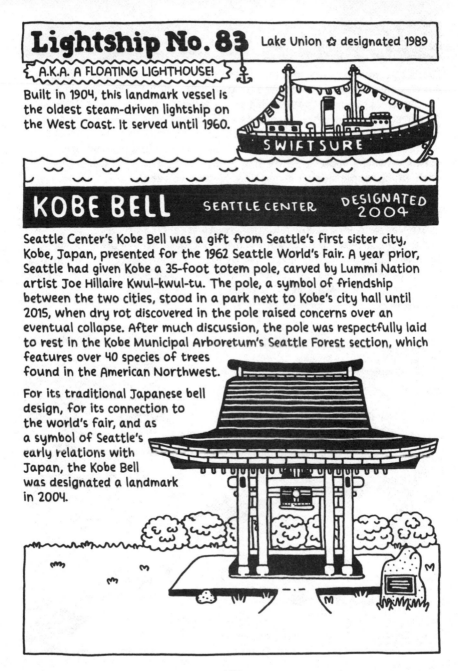

SWIFTSURE

KOBE BELL

SEATTLE CENTER

DESIGNATED 2004

Seattle Center's Kobe Bell was a gift from Seattle's first sister city, Kobe, Japan, presented for the 1962 Seattle World's Fair. A year prior, Seattle had given Kobe a 35-foot totem pole, carved by Lummi Nation artist Joe Hillaire Kwul-kwul-tu. The pole, a symbol of friendship between the two cities, stood in a park next to Kobe's city hall until 2015, when dry rot discovered in the pole raised concerns over an eventual collapse. After much discussion, the pole was respectfully laid to rest in the Kobe Municipal Arboretum's Seattle Forest section, which features over 40 species of trees found in the American Northwest.

For its traditional Japanese bell design, for its connection to the world's fair, and as a symbol of Seattle's early relations with Japan, the Kobe Bell was designated a landmark in 2004.

líq'təd (Licton) Springs *designated 2019*

For thousands of years, the spring in what is now called Licton Springs Park was a sacred site of ceremony and celebration for the Duwamish people, and known by Coast Salish tribes across the region as a source of prized red-ocher pigment, necessary for practices from prayer and healing to painting and trading. In the decades following the arrival of white settlers to the area in 1851, the rumored healing properties of the spring became a source of curiosity and interest among non-Natives, with white people visiting the spring, hoping to see the effects for themselves. With time, the spring's importance to the Duwamish people ran the risk of being lost to history.

In 2019, after a long Native-led grassroots effort to preserve and reclaim the sacred spring and its stories, Licton Springs Park became Seattle's first designated landmark of Native significance. It took nearly 50 years after the Seattle Landmarks Preservation Board was established in 1973 for this to happen.

How does something become a landmark?

In Seattle, anyone can submit a landmark nomination for a building or object that is at least 25 years old by filling out a nomination form that demonstrates the proposed landmark's significance, either historically, culturally, or architecturally. The nomination is reviewed at a public hearing in front of the Landmarks Preservation Board. If it passes that stage, another public hearing is held before the nomination heads to the Seattle City Council for a final vote.

My picks for future non-building landmarks

Bruce Lee Memorial Booth ☆ Tai Tung restaurant ☆ 655 S. King St.

This booth in the back of Chinatown-International District's Tai Tung restaurant was the seat of choice for martial arts master and actor Bruce Lee, who loved chowing down on garlic shrimp or oyster sauce beef.

Picardo Farm Community Garden
8040 25th Ave. NE

Food Bank Team.

Seattle's community garden program has roots in Picardo Farm. A successful experiment on this former family farm in 1973 led to the creation of a citywide "P-Patch" program the following year. There are now 89 official P-Patches throughout the city.

A working pay phone
Northgate Transit Center
140 NE 100th St.

Is your refrigerator running?

FOUR MILE ROCK

Puget Sound, at the foot of Magnolia Bluff

Magnolia's Four Mile Rock is so named because it was exactly four nautical miles away from early Seattle pioneer Henry Yesler's wharf, which was located where Downtown Seattle's ferry terminal now stands. Under this logic, I am going to proclaim that Medina's Overlake Golf and Country Club henceforth be called Four Mile Golf Course, as it is exactly four miles from where I personally live. The Duwamish people called the rock LE'plEpL or Tele'tla, a word for "rock" or "boulder." Whatever its name, this glacial erratic is a natural wonder that has loomed large near Magnolia Bluff for thousands of years.

A navigation marker sits atop the rock.

"FUN" ACTIVITY!

IT'S ALL RELATIVE!

You will need:

- ☐ an atlas
- ☐ a compass with a pencil
- ☐ something you *desperately* need to procrastinate over

① On a map, find the spot you call home.

② Making sure to consult the scale on your map, use your compass to draw a circle in a four-mile radius from where you live.

③ Declare anything on the edge of the circle YOUR "Four Mile ___"

④ Notify your friends and loved ones. Congratulations!

Want to meet at Four Mile Park?

Yours or mine?

Now I'm at NE 68th St. and Weedin Pl. NE, near Green Lake, where just below me is the site of a most unusual underground relic.

Nearly 30,000 people visited the Seattle World's Fair on May 15, 1962. Formally called the Century 21 Exposition, the fair, with its theme "living in the space age," celebrated an optimistic, technologically advanced vision of the future, complete with the atomic-cool Space Needle, a state-of-the-art monorail, the introduction of touch-tone telephones, and many Americans' first taste of Belgian waffles. But on the same day, only five miles away, a very different vision of the future was breaking ground.

ZAD!

ZOINKS! While fair attendees were chowing down on those Belgian waffles, construction was beginning on a federally funded fallout shelter under I-5, intended as a prototype to be replicated under interstate highways nationwide. The project was completed in 1963, but it was never used for its intended purpose and was never duplicated, making it the only fallout shelter to be built under a public highway in the United States. After a brief stint as a storage space for WSDOT, the shelter is now vacant.

BLEAK!

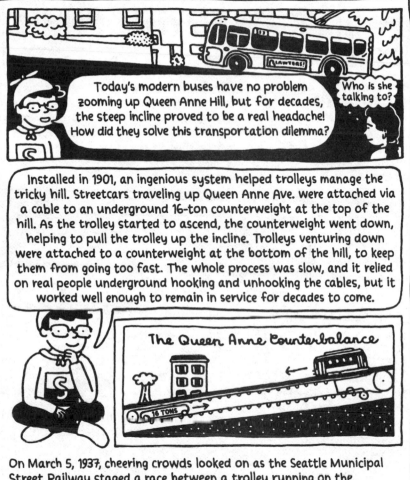

On March 5, 1937, cheering crowds looked on as the Seattle Municipal Street Railway staged a race between a trolley running on the counterbalance system and a new "trackless" trolley, intending to see which one could climb the hill the fastest. As the *Seattle Daily Times* recounted the following day, "The modern trackless coach embarrassed a Queen Anne street car last night, making the 2,150-foot hill in less than half the time required by the street car operated on the counterbalance." It would seem that the counterbalance's fate was sealed. The trackless trolley began its reign on Queen Anne Ave. in 1940, rendering the counterbalance obsolete, but the two counterbalance tunnels and their hefty counterweights are still in place.

TROLLEY HILL PARK

| 1800 Taylor Ave. N. | Queen Anne |

Along the eastern edge of Queen Anne Hill sits Trolley Hill Park, home to a pea-sized P-Patch community garden. The park's name was inspired by the popular trolley line that ran along nearby 5th Ave. N. from 1890 until 1940. If you'd like to extend your time in the great outdoors, the Northeast Queen Anne Greenbelt, accessible from the park, leads to MacLean Park, which offers a nice view of Puget Sound, the Cascades, and Gas Works Park. It's a park-a-palooza!

Soundview Terrace

| 2500 11th Ave. W. | Queen Anne |

Over on Queen Anne's western edge, Soundview Terrace is true to its name, with dazzling views of Puget Sound and Magnolia atop a steep hillside. It's the perfect spot for catching the sunset or catching a break. And while you're here, be sure to check out the cute tile art near the playground.

Seattle Brick Spotting

Everything you ever wanted to know about local bricks (but were afraid to ask!)

You can find them lurking in the city's P-Patches, hiding in small sidewalk gardens, or just hanging out in a ditch: they're loose stamped bricks, tiny pieces of forgotten history. Countless millions of bricks, many manufactured locally, went into constructing the Puget Sound's earliest buildings and roads, though most have been lost to time, dumped into landfills or buried under cement. But once you start looking for these clay curiosities, you may be surprised at how many you spot in locations across the city. In the small Thomas Street Gardens on Capitol Hill, for example, many old bricks stamped with the names of various brickmakers can be found lining the plots.

In its early days, Seattle was a timber town. After the Great Seattle Fire of 1889 proved that maybe it wasn't such a great idea to build an entire city largely of wood, city ordinances mandated that new buildings in the burned-down business district be made of brick or stone. Brick, due to its low cost and fire resistance, was a popular choice, and Seattle's brick boom began.

Denny-Renton Clay & Coal Company

Seattle settler Arthur A. Denny was quick to capitalize on the building-material choice of the new and improved Seattle, buying the Puget Sound Fire Clay Company in 1892 to establish the Denny Clay Company. The factory got its start producing brick pavers, used on many of Seattle's earliest brick-paved streets, including the intersection of Pike St. and 1st Ave., outside Pike Place Market. Visitors marveling at the famous market sign should also look down at the little pieces of clay history they are standing on.

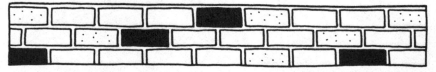

Even roads paved with asphalt were commonly lined with brick gutters, and many are still visible today. Like bricks themselves, brick gutters are another little thing that once you start noticing, you'll likely begin to see everywhere.

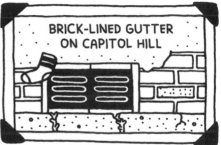

BRICK-LINED GUTTER ON CAPITOL HILL

In 1905, the Denny Clay Company merged with Renton Clay Works to become the Denny-Renton Clay and Coal Company, and a true Puget Sound powerhouse was born. By 1908, the massive kilns of their South King County factory could produce 250,000 paving bricks a day, making it the largest paving-brick plant in the United States.

By 1917, it was said that Denny-Renton was the largest producer of street-paving bricks in the entire world. Due to the company's cornering of the local brick game, the Denny-Renton name can be found stamped on bricks throughout Seattle, indicating that a brick is nearly a century old, if not older.

THE FRYE HOTEL

Though the company had built its fortunes on brick pavers, it went on to produce the bricks that would be used to construct many buildings still standing today, including Holy Names Academy, the Alaska Building, Franklin High School, the Frye Hotel, St. James Cathedral, and the West Seattle Library.

Denny-Renton also manufactured the terra-cotta for the Seattle Times Building, the King County Courthouse, and the walruses of the Arctic Building, making a lasting impression on the cityscape.

California-based Gladding, McBean bought the company in 1927 and ended operations under the Denny-Renton name. But across the city, their bricks endure.

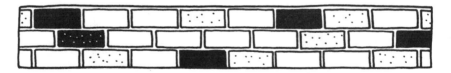

Brick Identification Guide

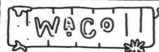

Washington Brick & Lime Co. "WaCo" bricks

↳ spotted in Capitol Hill

The Washington Brick and Lime Co. was a Spokane-based brick manufacturer with five clay plants across the state. Its facility in Clayton (a town named for its plentiful clay deposits) was the largest brick manufacturing plant in Eastern Washington at the time of its construction in 1893, and it produced bricks that went on to destinations across the Pacific Northwest. The "WaCo" stamp was used from the early 1920s until the company's acquisition by Gladding, McBean in 1957.

Gladding, McBean & Co. "Columbia" bricks

↳ spotted in the Central District

These bricks, manufactured by Gladding, McBean and Company, are stamped with "COLUMBIA" and a small oval "GMB C" logo. While the company got its start in brick and terra-cotta, it may be better known for its dinnerware. Ceramics fans will recognize Gladding McBean's essential contribution to midcentury dish design: the Franciscan Pottery "Starburst" line.

Look here! ↘

CITY LIGHT

Look there! →

Look everywhere! ↗

Carnegie Brick & Pottery Co.
"Carnegie" bricks

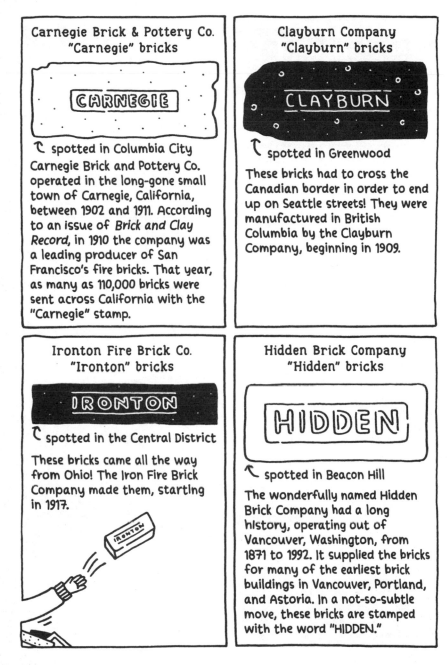

↪ spotted in Columbia City

Carnegie Brick and Pottery Co. operated in the long-gone small town of Carnegie, California, between 1902 and 1911. According to an issue of *Brick and Clay Record*, in 1910 the company was a leading producer of San Francisco's fire bricks. That year, as many as 110,000 bricks were sent across California with the "Carnegie" stamp.

Clayburn Company
"Clayburn" bricks

↪ spotted in Greenwood

These bricks had to cross the Canadian border in order to end up on Seattle streets! They were manufactured in British Columbia by the Clayburn Company, beginning in 1909.

Ironton Fire Brick Co.
"Ironton" bricks

↪ spotted in the Central District

These bricks came all the way from Ohio! The Iron Fire Brick Company made them, starting in 1917.

Hidden Brick Company
"Hidden" bricks

↪ spotted in Beacon Hill

The wonderfully named Hidden Brick Company had a long history, operating out of Vancouver, Washington, from 1871 to 1992. It supplied the bricks for many of the earliest brick buildings in Vancouver, Portland, and Astoria. In a not-so-subtle move, these bricks are stamped with the word "HIDDEN."

HIDDEN GEMS Boulevards

Cheasty Boulevard South

At just over one mile, this Beacon Hill boulevard is a delightful destination for an afternoon walk. The quiet, winding road is surrounded by a densely forested greenspace that can make you feel like you're the last person in Seattle. The boulevard has been a designated landmark since 2003.

Queen Anne Boulevard

This landmark boulevard is a scenic four-mile loop around the "crown" of Queen Anne. But you won't find a street named Queen Anne Blvd. on a map. Instead, the boulevard moniker is given to the series of streets that make up the loop, including W. Highland Dr., W. McGraw St., and Bigelow Ave. N. To follow the route, look for the special brown street signs.

On the boulevard, you'll pass by many dreamy houses, Mount Pleasant Cemetery (the final resting place for civil rights leader Bertha Pitts Campbell and longtime Seattle City Council member Sam Smith, among others), and the Willcox Wall, a unique old brick-and-concrete retaining wall and staircase with amazing views. Any way you look at it, you're bound to be charmed.

A dog's dream walk!

Terra-Cotta Treasures

Downtown Seattle is home to a secret animal kingdom, and all you need to do to find it is look up! The city is lucky to have many older buildings featuring expertly crafted ornamental terra-cotta, from the classical to the fanciful, including depictions of animal friends from land, sky, and sea. Between 1890 and 1940, terra-cotta became a popular choice for architects and builders: it was less expensive than stonework, versatile in form and shape, and more weather-resistant than other building materials available at the time. The result is a rich tapestry of flora and fauna cast in clay that has dazzled Seattleites for decades.

Walruses of the Arctic Building (1916) 700 3rd Ave.

Perhaps the most well-known terra-cotta animals in Seattle are the walruses of the Arctic Building, keeping a watchful eye on citizens since 1916. When the walruses made their grand debut, it marked the first time that a Downtown building used exterior color in terra-cotta, a cheery choice that stood in stark contrast to Seattle's gray skies. These marvelous mammals were originally manufactured by the Denny-Renton Clay and Coal Company. It can be difficult to stay in one place for over 100 years, but these walruses have certainly been up to the tusk!

Bulls of the Coliseum Theater (1916)
500 Pike St.

The Coliseum Theater, now home to clothing store Banana Republic, was one of the first theaters in the world designed and built specifically for the showing of motion pictures. This particular motif, which can be seen in a decorative band around the building, features bull heads, fruit, florals, and ribbons, a nod to ancient Greek and Roman sacrificial ceremonies, wherein cattle were decorated with elaborate garlands or ornamental ropes before their slaughter. It's a lot to think about while shopping for midpriced khakis, but it speaks to Coliseum architect B. Marcus Priteca's love of classical ornamentation.

Eagles of the Eagles Auditorium Building (1925)
1416 7th Ave.

The Fraternal Order of Eagles, an international nonprofit social club with over 800,000 members, began in Seattle in 1898 when six local theater owners had a meeting to discuss an ongoing musicians' strike. After deciding to unite with the musicians, they formed a group dedicated to mutual cooperation. As the group grew in Seattle and beyond in the years that followed, more space was needed to house meetings and other events. At seven stories tall, this building was the Eagles' grandest yet. The auditorium replaced Dreamland, a roller-skating rink turned dance hall that had resided on 7th and Union since 1907. Fittingly, this majestic terra-cotta eagle greeted members as they arrived with open ~~arms~~ wings. The building has been home to ACT Theatre since 1996.

UGH, my wings are TIRED!

SEATTLE AERIE No 1
FRATERNAL ORDER
· · · OF EAGLES · · ·

Lions of the Hoge Building (1911) 705 2nd Ave.

The entire 18-story steel frame for the Hoge Building roared to life in only 30 days, a speed unprecedented in Seattle during the time of construction. The building's financier, wealthy businessman John Hoge, was in a friendly competition with typewriter tycoon L. C. Smith to build the tallest building in the city. Hoge managed to hold the title and the glory only briefly before Smith's 35-story building opened. As a result, the Smith Tower didn't just become the tallest building in Seattle; it became the tallest skyscraper west of Ohio when it was completed in 1914. While today the Hoge Building is not as well-known as the Smith Tower, both exemplify popular styles of the time. The terra-cotta lion heads that grace the top floor of the Hoge Building, along with other architectural flourishes, make the building worth a visit.

Horse of Union Stables (1910) 2200 Western Ave.

Hayyy!

The decorative horse head on the front of Belltown's Union Stables building is the only clue to its original purpose as a humongous home for horses, with 300 stalls and an undoubtedly sky-high hay bill. At the time, it was seen as the most modern building of its kind west of Mississippi. These *neighhh*-bors played an important role in all aspects of city life, from drawing Seattle's fire engines and delivering newspapers to carting goods to and from nearby Pike Place Market. While reliance on horse-drawn vehicles faded as automobiles gained popularity, the building serves as an example of the urban horse stables that were once common in cities across the country.

Seattle Frieze!

Chamber of Commerce Building (1924)
215 Columbia St.

In architectural terms, a "frieze" is a decorative horizontal band typically located below the roofline, either inside or outside a building. On Columbia St.'s grand Chamber of Commerce Building, a terra-cotta frieze features animals native to Washington, including bears, pelicans, mountain goats, wild horses, and mountain lions.

BUILDING DOPPELGÄNGERS

Robbins Building (1927) 4538 University Way NE

Lewis Building (1931) 613 Broadway E.

These two buildings decorated with griffins, everyone's favorite mythological lion-eagle hybrid, are separated by four years and three miles, yet they are nearly identical! They were the work of prolific Seattle architect Henry W. Bittman, most famous for designing the Terminal Sales Building in Belltown.

Deadhorse Canyon

10201 Holyoke Way S. | Rainier Valley

The good news: Deadhorse Canyon in Lakeridge Park is a lovely sanctuary for wildlife and humans alike, where you can find quiet refuge only minutes away from busy Rainier Ave. S.

The bad news: you don't get a name like Deadhorse Canyon without at least one dead horse.

The story goes that the canyon got its name from a feral horse, beloved by pioneer children, that died on the land in the 1900s. However, the horse's memory lives on here, where raccoons and owls can be spotted alongside old-growth trees, walking paths, and a charming wooden bridge over Taylor Creek. It is one of South Seattle's best parks.

In Loving Memory

To celebrate the life of the unknown horse that gave Deadhorse Canyon its name, draw a horse living life to the fullest:

Ideas

Eating Dick's french fries at Kerry Park!

Proposing to another horse on the ferry to Bainbridge Island while we are forced to watch!

Trying to decide which lamp to buy for their Capitol Hill micro studio!

DIARY of a FIRE HYDRANT

Dear Diary,

Hey, it's me again, the Kennedy Valve Company's K81D Guardian model, the new kid on the block in Seattle's fire hydrant scene. To be honest, even though I'm the latest and greatest hydrant in Seattle right now, sometimes I feel invisible, you know? I guess that in a city with over 18,000 fire hydrants it can be hard to stand out, but I feel like people don't even notice me anymore. Like, sure, hydrants have been on Seattle's streets since the late 1880s, we're old news, blah, blah, blah. But like, we have feelings, too. If only people would take the time to look more closely, they would see that we're so much more than boring, indistinguishable vessels to help fight fires. We're each unique, like little cast-iron time capsules. Or at least that's what my mom says. Who knows.

Anyway, Diary. I've been meaning to share some photos of my fellow hydrants for a while, so that's what I'm going to do! I hope you like it.

me!

Go with the flow

about me:

Favorite color: Yellow

Favorite song: "Waterfalls" by TLC

Favorite movie: *Titanic*

HYDRANT PARTS

Here I am outside Fire Station 30 in Mount Baker (not my best angle, sooooooooooo embarrassing!)

TOTALLY ME! Ha ha!

operating nut — bonnet — outlet cap — barrel

BEE IN MY BONNET

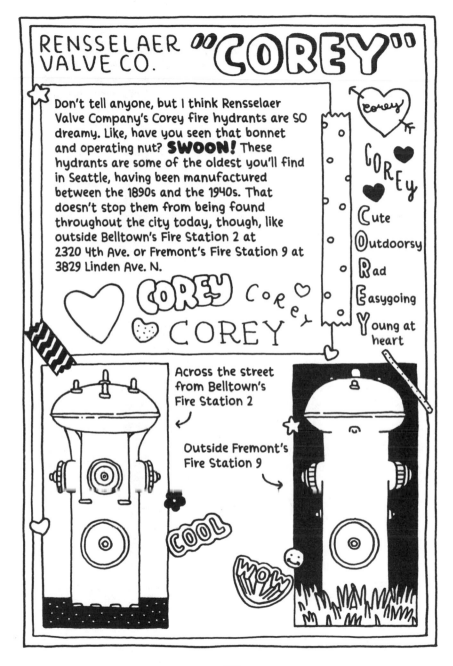

RENSSELAER VALVE CO. "COREY"

Don't tell anyone, but I think Rensselaer Valve Company's Corey fire hydrants are SO dreamy. Like, have you seen that bonnet and operating nut? **SWOON!** These hydrants are some of the oldest you'll find in Seattle, having been manufactured between the 1890s and the 1940s. That doesn't stop them from being found throughout the city today, though, like outside Belltown's Fire Station 2 at 2320 4th Ave. or Fremont's Fire Station 9 at 3829 Linden Ave. N.

Cute
Outdoorsy
Rad
Easygoing
Young at heart

Across the street from Belltown's Fire Station 2

Outside Fremont's Fire Station 9

COOL

WOW

IOWA VALVE CO. "IOWA"

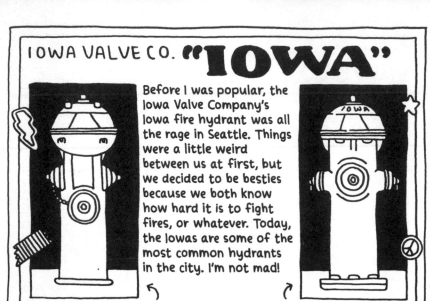

Before I was popular, the Iowa Valve Company's Iowa fire hydrant was all the rage in Seattle. Things were a little weird between us at first, but we decided to be besties because we both know how hard it is to fight fires, or whatever. Today, the Iowas are some of the most common hydrants in the city. I'm not mad!

Across the street from Fire Station 6 in the Central District

Outside Fire Station 16 in Green Lake

PACIFIC STATES CAST IRON PIPE CO. "M1" & "M2"

When my mom told me that these two very different-looking fire hydrants were related, I was like, "Whaaa?" But it's true. Both were manufactured by the Pacific States Cast Iron Pipe Company, which was established in Utah in 1926. These hydrants have the year that the hydrant was manufactured on the barrel, which is cool, I guess.

M1 model outside Fire Station 24 in Bitter Lake

M2 model outside Fire Station 25 in Capitol Hill

R. D. WOOD CO. "Mathews"

Me in my favorite hat

Have you ever met someone from the Philadelphia area? They CANNOT stop talking about Wawa, some convenience store chain there. If I hear one more word about those hoagie sandwiches, I am going to SCREAM! But East Coasters may be surprised to learn that some fire hydrants in Seattle have a connection to their beloved sandwich source. R. D. Wood Company began as an iron foundry in New Jersey in 1803, eventually getting into the fire hydrant business in the 1870s. The family business grew and diversified after World War II, opening a small milk-processing plant. Then in 1964, a descendant of the company's founder opened the first Wawa Food Market.

These beauties aren't very common, but they pop up in unexpected places, like this one at NW 80th St. and 11th Ave. NW in Greenwood.

TOO HOT TO HANDLE

WATER'S UP!

DIVA

KENNEDY ELMIRA, NY 175

COREY

Til next time,

♡ K81D Guardian

133

CAMP LONG

| 5200 35th Ave. SW | West Seattle |

Calling Camp Long—at 68 acres—a hidden gem feels like a stretch, yet compared to other spots like Discovery Park, Green Lake, and Seward Park, Camp Long doesn't seem to get the recognition it deserves among Seattleites outside of West Seattle. While the park was originally built exclusively for scouting groups, it has been open to the public since 1984, and it offers more than the average city park: There are cabins to rent and a ropes course. And then there's the 20-foot-high Schurman Rock. Named for Northwest mountaineer Clark Schurman and built in the late 1930s by the Works Progress Administration, it's believed to be the first artificial climbing structure in the United States.

For those who like to keep their adventures closer to the ground, Camp Long has several trails offering some of Seattle's best short nature walks. The flat Middle Loop Trail is the perfect way to admire big-leaf maples and alder trees while hoping to catch a glimpse of the eagles, hawks, and owls known to fly overhead. At Polliwog Pond in the late winter, an entire world is visible just below the water's surface as salamanders spring to life and tadpoles swim about. No matter the season, Camp Long is a great reason to get outside.

↙ Part of Schurman Rock

One of Camp Long's rentable cabins

SHIFTING BORDERS, STANDOUT BUILDINGS!

Over the course of single year, 1907, Seattle saw its population soar dramatically through annexation. Ballard, Columbia City, Ravenna, Southeast Seattle, South Park, and West Seattle all successfully petitioned to become another jewel in the crown of Seattle, the Queen City. By the year's end, Seattle had nearly doubled its land area and was looking less like a scruffy lumber-loving frontier town and more like the blossoming modern city it would become. Across these towns-turned-neighborhoods today, you can find structures that have stood the test of time, predating the big incorporation.

BALLARD est. 1890

At the turn of the century, Ballard was known as "The Shingle Capital of the World"—maybe not for the reason you think. The town was home to many mills that made roofing shingles.

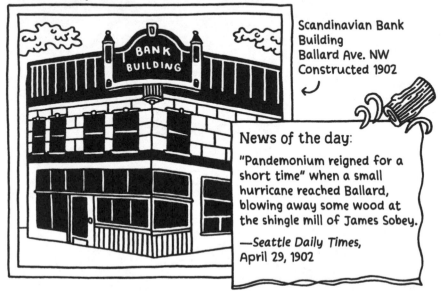

Scandinavian Bank Building
Ballard Ave. NW
Constructed 1902

News of the day:

"Pandemonium reigned for a short time" when a small hurricane reached Ballard, blowing away some wood at the shingle mill of James Sobey.

—*Seattle Daily Times,*
April 29, 1902

Columbia City est. 1892

Columbia City was a prosperous mill town before being annexed, served by a rail line that spanned from Downtown Seattle to the Rainier Valley. Annexation wasn't an easy choice: the town was proud to boast that it had no saloons within its limits, and many citizens felt that losing the ability to control the flow of alcohol would be detrimental to Columbia City's future. However, when the population continued to grow but infrastructure didn't, residents put their saloon concerns aside and voted to join Seattle.

Columbia Hotel
Rainier Ave. S.
Originally built: 1892
Expanded: 1904

News of the day:

Petty thieves "largely devoted to stealing small quantities of hay" caused concern for residents of Columbia City.

—*Seattle Daily Times*, November 19, 1897

Wasn't me!

RAVENNA est. 1906

Prior to annexation, one of Ravenna's biggest attractions was Ravenna Park. Seattleites would take the streetcar over Portage Bay and plunk down a quarter to marvel at the park's large trees, including a giant fir, which loomed large at nearly 400 feet high.

Residence
NE Naomi Pl.
Constructed 1905

Ravenna Park

News of the day:
A child ice-skating on a small pond near Ravenna Park broke through the ice, but the boy said "it was his day to take a bath anyway, so he saved a lot of time by taking it with his clothes on."

—*Seattle Daily Times,*
March 14, 1906

Southeast Seattle

Rainier Valley neighborhoods except Columbia City

·~· est. 1906 ·~·

The group of districts that made up the city of Southeast Seattle had been home to a railway line, a successful sawmill, and residential housing since the late 1800s, as real estate developers looking to make a profit from Seattle's growing population turned their sights to building opportunities to the south. The city is said to have incorporated solely for the purpose of petitioning for annexation.

Residence
S. Morgan St.
Constructed 1901

News of the day:

An advertisement for lots in Southeast Seattle's Hillman City proclaims: "HILLMAN CITY! HILLMAN CITY! THE PLACE WHERE THEY DO THINGS."

—*Seattle Daily Times*, April 20, 1903

(Hillman City's namesake, real estate developer Clarence Hillman, was most certainly doing "things"—after many years of shady business practices, he was indicted on charges of mail fraud in 1910.)

SOUTH PARK

est. 1902

Farmland and greenhouses were common sights in South Park, tended to by the Italian and Japanese immigrants that called the tiny town their home. Desire for a safer water supply and access to electrical utilities led South Park citizens to approve annexation, adding 1,500 new residents to Seattle.

Residence
10th Ave. S.
Constructed 1900

According to property records, before annexation the second floor of this house held South Park's town hall.

News of the day:

South Park resident Lizzie Coats, 18, was thrown a birthday party "in the nature of a surprise" at her parents' house.

—*Seattle Daily Times* February 9, 1902

In the early 1900s, South Park's produce couldn't be beet!

Booo!

West Seattle est. 1902

West Seattle was largely residential when talks of annexation began. Like in many other areas, water, transportation, and public safety issues were at the front of residents' minds as they debated whether or not to join Seattle. It may have been the opening of Luna Park along the northern tip of Alki that ultimately pushed locals to support the change: many feared that the amusement park would bring more riffraff and vice than carnival games and carousel rides, and they hoped Seattle would have the extra resources to deal with the coming scourge. Residents voted in favor of annexation two days after Luna Park opened its doors.

Mixed-use building
California Ave. SW
Constructed 1905
↙

News of the day: Young Marie Bernard of Alki Point "narrowly escaped death" as the ramp to board the steamer *Dix* collapsed, taking the child with it. Fortunately, she was uninjured. Months later, the *Dix* company presented her with a lifetime pass and a silver medal with a picture of the steamer engraved on it. The lifetime pass didn't last long: tragically, a year and a half later, the *Dix* sank in a collision.

—*Seattle Daily Times*, February 28, 1905

HIDDEN GEMS

Sunset Hill Park

7531 34th Ave. NW	Ballard

On a bluff in the northwest corner of Ballard sits this small park and overlook, where you can feel the breeze while enjoying spectacular views of Shilshole Bay and the Olympic Mountains. It is named for the community that surrounds it and, of course, for its spectacular sunsets.

UNSOLVED MUNDANE HISTORICAL MYSTERY?

It's a cloudy day in February 1923, and the Sunset Hill Improvement Club is having its twice-monthly meeting at Webster Elementary School. On the agenda is an item of utmost interest to club members far and wide: What should they select for their all-important community flower, the one that will help them reach their goal of making Sunset Hill the most attractive neighborhood in all of Seattle?

After what could only be a spirited discussion, gladioluses are selected. "Residents of the district will plant gladioluses by the thousands and, in the future, Sunset Hill will be known as the place where the gladioluses bloom in profusion," wrote the *Seattle Daily Times*. Yet two months later, at the group's late April meeting, the news breaks that the club has adopted the red geranium as the community flower instead, and the once-revered gladiolus is never mentioned again.

Long-form essay question: Why did Seattle's Sunset Hill Improvement Club turn on the gladiolus flower in favor of the red geranium so quickly in spring of 1923? Was it something that the gladioluses said? Is it because the red geranium is way prettier and everyone knows it? Write your theory here. Use complete sentences.

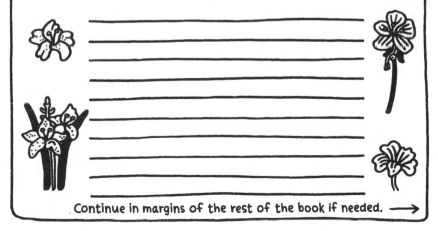

Continue in margins of the rest of the book if needed. ⟶

Cheshiahud Lake Union Loop 6 miles, established 2008

Entry point: Lake Union Park, 860 Terry Ave. N.

CHESHIAHUD

The Cheshiahud Lake Union Loop was named for Cheshiahud, leader of a Duwamish village on what we now call Lake Union. Cheshiahud and his family were the last of the Duwamish people who had originally inhabited the area around the lake to live there, maintaining a small cabin and potato patch near Portage Bay.

With many points of interest along the way, like the Museum of History and Industry, houseboats, the Fremont Bridge, and Gas Works Park, the mostly flat loop is a great way for visitors or newcomers to the city to get acquainted with Seattle, while still offering plenty for seasoned Seattleites.

Terminal 91 Bike Path 3.5 miles, established 1987

Entry point: Centennial Park, 2711 Alaskan Way

The Elliott Bay Trail along the waterfront includes the 3.5-mile Terminal 91 Bike Trail. Initiated, financed, and designed by the Port of Seattle, the bike trail weaves through industrial loading areas and railroad yards. Prior to its creation, bicyclists heading north needed to brave a ride over railroad tracks and through the heavy traffic of 15th Ave. W. Whether you're on wheels or on foot, it's an interesting glimpse into industrial Seattle, with the bonus of access to Myrtle Edwards Park, the Olympic Sculpture Park, and the Magnolia neighborhood.

Discovery Park > 12 miles of trails, established in 1973

Entry point: W. Emerson St. & Magnolia Blvd. W.

For the ancestral Duwamish, Muckleshoot, and Suquamish peoples, the land that is now Seattle's largest park was a place of discovery for thousands of years. Archaeologists say that mussels, periwinkles, elk, and deer were among the area's many offerings. But it was a different sort of discovery that this park was named for: it comes from the ship *Discovery*, which British commander Captain George Vancouver used during his expedition mapping the Pacific coast in the 1790s. Names for many of the region's natural places can be traced to this expedition, including Puget Sound, Mount Rainier, Mount Saint Helens, and Whidbey Island.

The current park site was selected for an army base in the 1890s, and Fort Lawton opened in 1900, serving as a military post for decades before the majority of the land was turned over to the city, which turned it into a public park. Discovery Park offers great hiking and walking trails with a variety of scenic views, ranging from forest and open meadows to beach and sea. Plus, who doesn't love a good lighthouse?

Discovery Park is also home to the Daybreak Star Indian Cultural Center (pages 50 and 51), located on Bernie Whitebear Way, a street named for the Native American activist who fought for the center's creation.

Chief Sealth Trail > 3.5 miles, established 2007

Entry point: 15th Ave. S. and S. Angeline St.

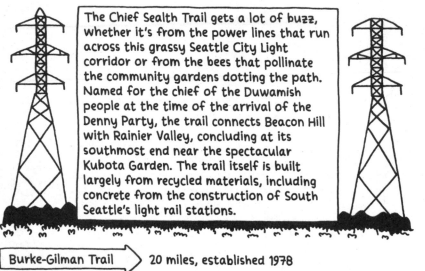

The Chief Sealth Trail gets a lot of buzz, whether it's from the power lines that run across this grassy Seattle City Light corridor or from the bees that pollinate the community gardens dotting the path. Named for the chief of the Duwamish people at the time of the arrival of the Denny Party, the trail connects Beacon Hill with Rainier Valley, concluding at its southmost end near the spectacular Kubota Garden. The trail itself is built largely from recycled materials, including concrete from the construction of South Seattle's light rail stations.

Burke-Gilman Trail > 20 miles, established 1978

Entry point: Shilshole Bay

One of Seattle's first railway lines used to roll across part of the route of today's Burke-Gilman Trail, named for two of the citizens instrumental in the railway's creation in the 1880s. When the railway owners looked to sell in 1971, the city sought to acquire the right-of-way and ultimately made a deal to exchange industrial property elsewhere in Seattle for the corridor. Interest in creating a bike path along the tracks had been growing for years, and officials seized their opportunity.

Not all residents living along the site of the proposed trail were happy, fearing that it would decrease property values while increasing crime and nuisance. After years of discussion, debate, and concessions on both sides, the trail was dedicated in 1978 and has since become the most beloved bike and pedestrian trail in the city. When you catch glimpses of Mount Rainier and Lake Washington along the way, it's easy to see why.

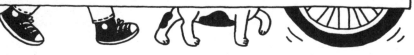

Azalea Way ⟩ 0.75 miles, established in the late 1930s

Entry point: Washington Park Arboretum, 2300 Arboretum Dr. E.

As you delight in the flowers and foliage along the Arboretum's Azalea Way path, it can be hard to believe that the land has ever been anything other than a quiet refuge. The Duwamish people had a village east of what is now Arboretum Creek, and they relied heavily on the land as well as its access to nearby waterways. By the 1890s, the land was regularly logged and the path of present-day Azalea Way served as a logging road. Later, the sound of skidding logs was replaced with the clip-clop of horse hooves after the city acquired the land, and the road became a speedway for horse races.

Azalea Way as we know it today came to fruition thanks to funding and labor from the Works Progress Administration, thousands of azaleas planted by the Seattle Garden Club, and the vision of the Olmsted Brothers landscape architecture firm, which saw the road's potential as a beautiful promenade. Azalea Way's namesake flower is typically in full bloom around April and May, along with rhododendrons, but the path is worth a visit year-round. Fortunately, these days you are unlikely to get bowled over by a racehorse or a skidding log.

Natural Areas

Union Bay Natural Area: 3501 NE 41st St.

This natural area near UW is a wonderful example of how you can turn trash into treasure. Once home to the city's largest garbage dump (and the purported home of local children's television character J. P. Patches between 1958 and 1981), the land is now a 74-acre public wildlife area, with walking paths, grasslands, and wetlands. It's a great spot for bird-watching.

Wolf Creek Ravine Natural Area: McGraw St., between 2nd Ave. N. & Nob Hill Ave. N.

Unlike some of Seattle's other natural areas, the Wolf Creek Ravine is mostly inaccessible, yet it's still a neat nature gem to find in the middle of a residential neighborhood. Admire the nearby Queen Anne P-Patch Community Garden before walking over the McGraw Street Bridge and appreciating the abundance of greenery below. Continue your bridge journey by heading north and checking out the landmark North Queen Anne Drive Bridge, built in 1936.

Home of Seattle's most ambivalent sign!

DUMP NO MATERIAL
WHATEVER
VIOLATORS ARE SUBJECT
TO
FINE AND ARREST
ORDINANCE
90047

Pelly Place Natural Area: 6762 Murray Ave. SW

This West Seattle natural area is named for a road that was to be part of a small housing development proposed at this site in the late 1980s. Neighbors were furious at the prospect of losing the wooded ravine here. Families held garage sales and children sold Christmas wreaths door-to-door to raise money for legal fees, and a land-use specialist working for the City of Seattle at the time said that the resulting paperwork was "one of the thickest files I've had in my 28 years here." In the end, the developers lost, and the result is a forested one-acre neighborhood treasure with a short trail.

Longfellow Creek Natural Area: Delridge Way SW & SW Graham St.

This beautiful natural area in Southwest Seattle boasts wooden footbridges, walking paths, a salmon stream, and interesting public art inspired by the nature that surrounds it.

History Happened Here

 Musicians Ray Charles and Quincy Jones meet for the first time
S. Jackson St., between Maynard Ave. S. and 7th Ave. S.

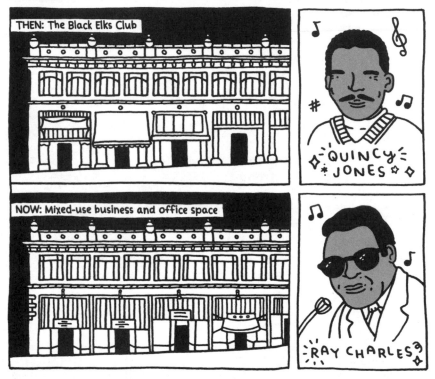

THEN: The Black Elks Club

NOW: Mixed-use business and office space

QUINCY JONES

RAY CHARLES

Between the 1930s and 1950s, the center of jazz music in Seattle was on Jackson St., where a burgeoning nightlife scene of over two dozen clubs attracted local and national acts and the jazz hounds who loved them. Despite the racial segregation prevalent at the time, the clubs of Jackson St. were a rare space where people of all races and socioeconomic backgrounds gathered, and the mostly Black musicians often played to diverse crowds. The Black Elks Club on the second floor of the Rainier Heat and Power Building was one of the clubs, and it was here that young Seattleite Quincy Jones first met an unknown teenage musician from Florida named R. C. Robinson, later known as Ray Charles. Thus began a friendship that would last a lifetime.

The first "permanent" home of the Seattle Public Library opens the doors to its reading room

Triangular piece of land bordered by 2nd Ave., James St., and Yesler Way

THEN: The Occidental Building

NOW: Parking garage

While valiant efforts to establish a public library in Seattle had been in motion as early as 1868, it would be another 23 years before the first "permanent" home of the Seattle Public Library opened the doors to its new reading room on the fifth floor of the elegant Occidental Building in Pioneer Square on April 8, 1891.

The library moved a few years later, and the Occidental Building served many other uses before falling into disrepair. Damage from an earthquake in 1949, followed by a partial collapse in 1961, compelled the city to demolish the building, replacing it with a parking lot that became derisively known as "the Sinking Ship." This set off alarm bells for architects, professors, preservationists, and everyday citizens, many of whom feared that the days of Seattle's historic buildings would be numbered if development were left unchecked. When the Seattle City Council adopted a plan aimed at revitalizing Downtown Seattle in 1963 that called for turning much of Pioneer Square into a giant parking lot, those fears gained a new sense of urgency. Through the efforts of a grassroots movement, Pioneer Square was designated as a national historic district in 1970, and later, as Seattle's first preservation district. Eventually, most of the grand plans to redevelop the neighborhood were scrapped.

Of course, in true Seattle fashion, everything is cool once enough time has passed: in 2019, architecture publication *Architizer* named the once-loathed Sinking Ship "the coolest parking garage in the United States."

First bicycle sold in Seattle
1st Ave. between Cherry St. and Yesler Way

On November 18, 1879, one lucky Seattle boy became the proud owner of not just the first bike on the block, in the neighborhood, or even in the entire city, but in ALL OF WASHINGTON TERRITORY, when his father, Jules Lipsky, bought the wheeled wonder from merchant William H. Pumphrey, owner of a stationery shop at 617 1st Ave. (then called Front St.), now a parking lot.

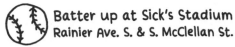

Batter up at Sick's Stadium
Rainier Ave. S. & S. McClellan St.

THEN: Sick's Stadium

NOW: Lowe's Home Improvement

Before the Kingdome or ~~Safeco Field~~ T-Mobile Park, Seattle had Sick's Stadium, a baseball park named for Rainier Brewery owner Emil Sick, which was home to the Seattle Rainiers and the short-lived Seattle Pilots. The ballpark was met with much fanfare in its early years, and had enthusiastic attendance to match, as the Rainiers batted their way to several minor league baseball championships. However, as the city grew, so, too, did its major league ambitions. Aging Sick's Stadium would have needed significant and costly improvements to be viable for the type of team the city hoped to attract. And when voters approved a 1968 bond to fund the Kingdome, the fate of the old ballpark was clear. After a brief life as a concert venue, attracting acts like Jimi Hendrix and Janis Joplin, by 1979 it was nothing but rubble. While today you're (hopefully) unlikely to hear the roar of a crowd or the crack of a bat in the hardware store that replaced the ballpark, for a generation of Seattle baseball fans, sweet memories of Sick's Stadium linger there.

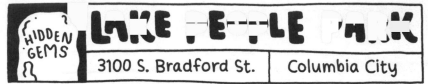

LAKE PEOPLE PARK

| 3100 S. Bradford St. | Columbia City |

Less than two decades ago, the current home of Columbia City's Lake People Park was simply a bluff of land above Rainier Ave. S. overrun with blackberry brambles. Now, it's a small refuge featuring benches, a picnic table, mossy stairs, native plants, and an assortment of medium-sized boulders sure to please any medium-sized boulder enthusiast.

NAME NOTE:

Lake People Park got its name from the word X̌acuabš, one of the names the Duwamish people historically used to refer to themselves in their ancestral language, Lushootseed. It means "People of the Large Lake" or "Lake People," referring to the group of Duwamish who lived near the body of water we now call Lake Washington.

CONCLUSION

There is practically no end to Seattle's secrets for those eager to uncover them. If you're inspired by tales of coal chutes and cluster lights, and want to learn more about the history and mystery in your own neck of the woods, the first step is to take a closer look at your environment. Pretend you're a detective who has been sent on a fact-finding mission about your neighborhood and try to forget everything you know about your surroundings, as though you've never been there before. What do you notice? Look high, low, close-up, and at a distance, paying attention to anything that catches your eye. Try simply observing the contours of your street without judgment. What do the houses or buildings look like? Do they look similar or different? What is the pattern on your nearest utility cover? It may take time to get used to this way of seeing, but with practice, you may be surprised at what previously overlooked parts of the cityscape come into view.

If you see something that sparks your interest and want to learn more, it can be daunting to know where to begin. Here are a few recommendations to help the amateur historian get started, all available online.

The *Seattle Times* Historical Archive

The *Seattle Times* archive is a digitized and searchable database of the newspaper and typically the first place I go when doing research. Best of all, it's accessible for free if you have a Seattle Public Library card! I will search for an address, a company name, a person's name, a phrase, or whatever little piece of information I have and see what results await. Remember to put your search term in quotation marks if you want to match an exact phrase. For example, "Fremont Bridge" has just over 5,000 results as of writing, whereas Fremont Bridge without quotations has nearly 50,000! Prepare to go down some serious rabbit holes.

Available at spl.org under "Online Resources"

Washington Digital Newspapers

The newspapers available online through the Washington State Library are primarily useful when researching pre-1900 Seattle history, as the majority of the newspapers in this archive are from that time period. Newspapers like the *Seattle Post-Intelligencer* from 1888 to 1900, the *Seattle Star* from 1899 to 1930, and the *Puget Sound Dispatch* from 1871 to 1880 are available for your perusing pleasure.

Available at washingtondigitalnewspapers.org

SEATTLE HISTORICAL SITES SEARCH from the Seattle Department of Neighborhoods

This resource pulls together information about some of the city's buildings and houses from old property records, directories, and other sources, making it a great way to get background information on Seattle structures. My favorite is the "Search by Property Attribute" option, where you can select a neighborhood and a year or date range and see all the property listings that meet your criteria.

Available at web6.seattle.gov/DPD/HistoricalSite

In the 1970s, Seattle Parks Department employee Don Sherwood undertook a major effort to ensure the preservation of materials related to city park history. The result is the Don Sherwood Parks History Collection, an excellent resource for learning more about Seattle's many parks and playfields. Files typically have a hand-drawn map alongside an overview of the park's history, including important dates and figures in the park's development.

Available at seattle.gov/cityarchives/search-collections/don-sherwood-park-history-sheets

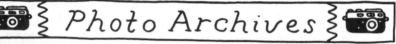

Photo Archives

The Seattle Public Library, the Museum of History and Industry, and the University of Washington all have great online historic photo archives. Sometimes, photo captions will give you additional crumbs of information that can help you continue your search.

Available at spl.org, mohai.org, and content.lib.washington.edu

Most importantly, if you learn something cool, share it with others! You may just become Seattle's best-kept secret.

Seattle Dog's-Eye View
with Bella the Bichon Frise

Hi, my name is Bella, which completely coincidently was one of Seattle's top dog names in 2019, along with Charlie, Luna, and Max. No one ever bothers to ask me about my interests, but I'll have you know that I enjoy avant-garde jazz, long walks in the city, and landscape architecture. Due to my stellar credentials, I've been asked to finish out this book by providing some insider tips that can help you better appreciate your surroundings.

Outdoor Identification Guide

By knowing the delightful names of infrastructure and other elements in your environment, you can describe your city like a pro!

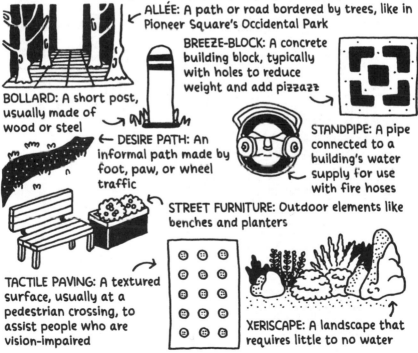

ALLÉE: A path or road bordered by trees, like in Pioneer Square's Occidental Park

BREEZE-BLOCK: A concrete building block, typically with holes to reduce weight and add pizzazz

BOLLARD: A short post, usually made of wood or steel

DESIRE PATH: An informal path made by foot, paw, or wheel traffic

STANDPIPE: A pipe connected to a building's water supply for use with fire hoses

STREET FURNITURE: Outdoor elements like benches and planters

TACTILE PAVING: A textured surface, usually at a pedestrian crossing, to assist people who are vision-impaired

XERISCAPE: A landscape that requires little to no water

Want a date? Seattle's infrastructure has clues that can help you figure out when certain things around you were manufactured or installed.

DATES ON SEATTLE DEPARTMENT OF TRANSPORTATION SIGNS: Many Seattle street signs have a small date printed on the bottom that shows when the sign was manufactured. Typically, the year is followed by the month in a two-digit format. Newer signs have the full year.

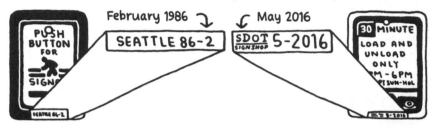

February 1986 → SEATTLE 86-2

May 2016 → SDOT SIGN SHOP 5-2016

DATE NAILS: There is a long-standing practice of nailing "date nails" to utility poles to indicate the year the poles were put in place. While some have gone missing over the years, many intact nails can be found throughout the city.

Sometimes I need to stand on my hind legs for this one!

95
1995 ↗

78
1978 ↗

GOLDEN OLDIE!

39

A 1939 date nail can be found near S. Dearborn St. and 19th Ave. S.! Seattle's population has doubled since this utility pole was installed.

WOODEN SIGNPOSTS: Around 2001, Seattle phased out wooden signposts in favor of metal posts, due to the increased cost of cedar posts from Canada. Look for the fun striped, candy-cane-like wooden stop-sign posts. They ↗ are at least 20 years old.

Utility Spray-Paint Mark Guide

You can't go far in Seattle without encountering a sea of spray paint on the pavement, with a swirl of colors, symbols, and letters that are inscrutable to the untrained eye. However, for the city's many utility and construction workers, this code delivers important messages about what lies under the streets and helps prevent the disasters that can erupt with careless digging. To everyone else, knowing the code is a fun way to win friends and learn a little more about the city's underground infrastructure.

Get to know the safety color code

WOOOO!

Different utilities are identified by a specific color of spray-paint:

	Red: Electric		Green: Sewers and drain lines
	Yellow: Gas, oil, fuel, and other flammables		Purple: Non-drinking water
	Orange: Cable, TV, telephone		Pink: Temporary survey marks
	Blue: Drinking water		White: Proposed excavation marks

Common symbols and their meanings

←SPU

Name of utility line owner (in this case, Seattle Public Utilities)

Location of underground utility line

End point of utility line

Indicates underground valves or manholes

Underground conduit

PSE ↑ 15°

In instances where the spray-paint marker can't be placed directly over the underground line, this line with an arrow indicates the line owner and the distance to the line. In this case, Puget Sound Energy's line is 15 feet away.

Used when the utility line has a large diameter

Fancy two-way arrow

LOCATION GUIDE

RAFFLE
PRIZE: ONE MANSION

Downtown & Belltown	5, 31, 32, 42, 43, 60-63, 64-65, 86-89, 90-91, 93, 95, 106, 125, 126, 127, 144
Eastlake & South Lake Union	32, 68, 72-75, 77, 107, 144
Fremont, Wallingford, & Green Lake	16-19, 30, 66, 68, 77, 94, 114
Leschi, Madrona, & Montlake	4, 12, 49, 54, 55, 67, 79, 147
Magnolia	50-51, 110-111, 145
Pioneer Square	8, 11, 60-63, 98-101, 124, 151, 152

Queen Anne	Lower: 2, 5, 30, 57, 58, 107 Upper: 4, 10, 20, 93, 95, 115, 116-117, 123, 148
Rainier Valley	20, 52-53, 70, 78, 81, 96-97, 128-129, 137, 139, 146, 153, 154-155
Ravenna, Wedgwood, & Northgate	55, 71, 76, 94, 109, 138
SoDo, Harbor Island, & Georgetown	3, 30, 32, 58, 92, 95
South Park	36-39, 140
University District	34, 35, 82-83, 127, 146, 148
West Seattle	14-15, 46-47, 55, 57, 59, 66, 68, 69, 71, 76, 92, 94, 134-135, 141, 149

Susanna Ryan is the author of the book *Seattle Walk Report: An Illustrated Walking Tour through 23 Seattle Neighborhoods*. She enjoys sighing and looking out windows when she's not on a neighborhood stroll.

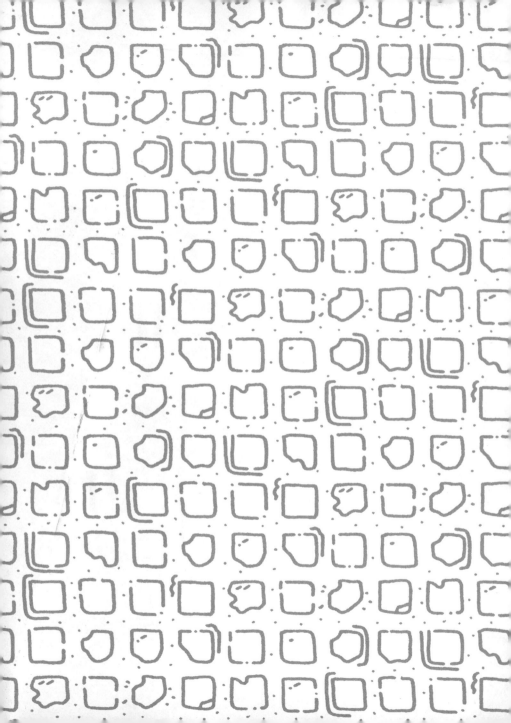